DESPERATELY SEEKING MARIE PREVOST

Richard Kirby

Desperately Seeking Marie Prevost
By Richard Kirby
© 2014, Richard Kirby. All Rights Reserved.
No part of this book may be reproduced in any form or by any means, electronic, mechanical, digital, photocopying or recording, except for the inclusion in a review, without permission in writing from the publisher. All photos are used in editorial fashion with no intention of infringement of intellectual property rights.

Published in the USA by:
BearManor Media
P O Box 71426
Albany, Georgia 31708
www.bearmanormedia.com

ISBN: 978-1-59393-574-0
Printed in the United States of America
Book design by Robbie Adkins

ACKNOWLEDGEMENTS

THANK YOU. . . .To Ben, Michelle, Wendy, Robbie and everyone at *BearManor Media* for their help and support—and wanting to work with me twice!

THANK YOU. . . .To Michelle Morgan (again!) for the initial inspiration for this book.

THANK YOU. . . .To me, for allowing me to use photographs, scans of pages from magazines, postcards and cigarette cards and stills from DVDs that I have purchased and therefore deem that I own.

THANK YOU. . . .To everyone who has read any of my work, especially those of you who parted with money to do so. I am genuinely both humbled and grateful.

THANK YOU. . . .To my wife Elaine, love you loads xx.

THANK YOU. . . .To my family and close friends, but especially my Mum and Dad, Anna and David, who celebrated their golden wedding anniversary in August 2013. I love you and this book is for you xx.

CONTENTS

Acknowledgements III

Introduction VII

Let the Confusion Begin 1

Sinful Pride, Enormous Guilt 5

Gerke the Jerky 13

The Flapper 25

A Very Taxing Time 37

What's the Frequency, Kenneth? 53

Kicking Up a Racket 59

Depression Sets In 67

Up in Smoke 77

The Last Pie 83

A Wonderful Friend 91

On Reflection 95

Bibliography & Sources 99

INTRODUCTION

Relatively hot on the heels—well, reasonably warm, at least—of my book about *Doctor Who*'s female companions, comes my second *BearManor Media* offering: a look back at the life of the Hollywood silent actress Marie Prevost.

Both titles begin "Desperately Seeking," which I would like to suggest—both prematurely and self-indulgently—is the start of a series in the making, but clearly there is a fundamental difference between the two volumes. Not to put too fine a point on it, my attempts at contacting actresses who had appeared in *Doctor Who* relied heavily on them being alive, whereas Marie Prevost passed away as long as go as 1937.

So the "seeking" this time is concerned with finding out what I can about Marie, and trying to understand just a little bit about her—and her life. This is undoubtedly a bit of a departure for me, but I have done as much research as I can—and fifty-something sources are referenced at the end of the book—in an attempt to separate likely fact from the more obvious fiction and put together a chronicle that is as accurate as possible.

I don't write for recognition—albeit I love receiving genuinely positive comments, perhaps more so from people who don't know me and yet have been willing to acquire a book based purely on recommendation, the subject-matter, my writing style, or most likely a mistaken click on the "BUY" button—and believe me, this hobby does nothing to swell the bank balance, I just enjoy the whole idea of discovering about a person, or an event, compiling the text as I learn, and ultimately holding a book in my hand as some tangible proof of my efforts.

I must also add that I don't regard my work as definitive in any way, I see this particular volume simply as an introduction to the life and times of Marie Prevost, which will hopefully be enjoyable in its own right, but may just leave the reader wanting to discover more.

Marie Prevost may well be a relatively new name to many, but during the mid- to late 1920s, she was one of the most feted stars of the big screen. Her life would ultimately come to a premature and desperately sad end, but how often does a story become more interesting for that very reason?

LET THE CONFUSION BEGIN

Well, the subject of separating truth from fiction mentioned in the introduction doesn't take long to rear its head: right from the outset, in fact, with Marie's date of birth.

I unearthed a number of sources that stated Mary Dunn was born in the city of Sarnia—which lies on the southern tip of Lake Huron in Ontario, Canada—on November 8, 1898.

But she wasn't.

Most sources suggested her middle name was "Bickford."

Which it wasn't—probably!

The birth record of the future Hollywood star (which was first posted on *The Gone Too Soon Blogathon: Marie Prevost on the site shebloggedbynight.com* in March 2012) shows that Marie Dunn entered the world on (Saturday) November 8, 1896, and, at some stage in her life, it was presumably decided that wiping two years off her age was a good move—and youth was usually an advantage for any would-be movie actress.

Marie's father is named as Arthur Dunn, a railway worker of Scottish extraction, and her mother is Hughina Dunn (née McDonald), who perhaps unsurprisingly also had Scottish roots. The couple married on September 25, 1895—when Hughina was just sixteen—and Marie was their only daughter.

Hughina was born in Ontario, in the registration district of Bruce Township to be more precise, to Archibald and Mary (née McGillivray) on June 3, 1879: thereby sharing a birthday with the author in the process.

The Bickford "confusion" may stem from the fact that the Christian name Hughina—which seems fairly uncommon (I had certainly never come across the name before)—was the middle name of one Mary Bickford, who was also born in Ontario, but a few years earlier than Hughina McDonald.

According to the 1881 census, ten-year-old Mary was living with her American-born parents Charles and Adeline—spelt Adaline in the 1891 census—whose ages were given as forty-seven and fifty respectively.

However, Marie *did* have a middle name, and whilst I'm no graphologist—and I struggle deciphering handwriting as well—I did take the time to study an enlargement of the birth registration, and concluded thus: The first letter is not a "B," and there is an example to compare. That said the last four letters do look like "ford." I've seen a number of stabs at the name: "Vicford"—the "i" in Marie has a dot in the ledger, but the second letter of her middle name doesn't—and "Vucford"—possible, but not exactly an everyday name.

If you twisted my arm, I'd go for the latter—maybe. . . .

Perhaps it's a simple transcription error, but whatever Marie's middle name actually was, I don't think it was Bickford. And whilst it is always possible there may have been some family link between the Bickfords and the McDonalds, what is apparent is that Mary Hughina Bickford and Marie Dunn were very much two different people, and as there is no evidence to the contrary, "Bickfordgate" ends here.

However, there is plenty more to add regarding the discrepancy over Marie's date of birth, and with a *New York Times* extract from November 30, 1897, comes a tragic ending that signaled the start of a journey that would eventually lead all the way to Hollywood.

On November 29, three train workers were killed as a result of an incident in the Grand Trunk Railway tunnel, which linked Port Huron, Michigan, with Canada. According to the short article, the train broke in two, and although the engine reversed down the tunnel in an effort to recover the separated part of the train, nothing was heard for several hours. A search party was deployed, and the bodies of Henry J. Courtney, engineer; Arthur Dunn, conductor; and John Dalton, brakeman were recovered: all three had died from asphyxiation.

Two members of the crew—William Dunn, fireman, and William Potter, brakeman—were recovered alive but unconscious, and three members of the recovery team were overcome by gas fumes and had to be carried out of the tunnel.

Awful—and there's not really a great deal more that needs to be added. . . .

Except that if Marie Dunn had indeed been born in November 1898, one of the following must be true: Arthur was not her father—and it has been conclusively proven that he was—Hughina's pregnancy lasted almost a whole year, or she was born sometime earlier.

The limited writings about Marie Dunn—Prevost to be—include *Stardust and Shadows* by Charles Foster. This book, published in 2000, takes an in-depth look at the lives of a number of Canadians who graced the big screen in the early days of the Hollywood movie industry.

In the chapter dedicated to Marie, Foster states that Marie lost her father when "she was only six" years of age, following the death of her railroad car conductor father Arthur—and from a few pages earlier: "Marie Prevost was born Mary Bickford Dunn on November 8 1898."

Well, the 1897 passing of Arthur Dunn is indisputable, yet within the space of a few paragraphs, Foster reckons that Mary [sic] was born in 1898, and then infers she was blowing out six candles on a birthday cake *before* she'd even been born.

In Foster's defense, the magazines of the day were no more accurate. Witness this repose to the question of Marie's age posed by Bobby from Chicago in an issue of *Photoplay* from early 1925: "This from undisputed authorities will, I hope, lower the temperature of the argument. She [*Marie*] was born in 1898."

There's no way of knowing how old Bobby was when he wrote to *Photoplay*, but he gets an honorable mention because the likelihood is that nearly ninety years on he's no longer with us, thereby allowing me to avoid the shattering blow of eventual revelation.

In actual fact, I did see another weekly claim that Marie was born in 1902! As you will soon discover, this would have made her younger than her younger sister—although somewhat fortuitously, her sister became an actress and lied about her age too.

After losing her husband, Hughina would soon leave her native Canada. By the time the 1900 US census was taken—the Twelfth Census of the United States was conducted on June 1, 1900—Hughina was living in Ouray City, Colorado; she had married a gentleman named Frank Prevost, and the couple also had a two-month old daughter, who they had named Marjorie.

The census extract gives Hughina's year of birth as 1871—the same year as Mary Hughina Bickford was born (I was evidently wrong about "Bickfordgate" being over)—yet it has already been demonstrated that Hughina McDonald, then Dunn, now Prevost, was born in 1879.

Not sure I'm going to get to the bottom of this one. Hughina was already eighteen by the time she was widowed, so she wouldn't have transgressed any laws for the legal minimum age to wed in Canada (seeing as she'd already been married) or Colorado.

However, what is clear is that Marie and Marjorie were half- and not full sisters. Marjorie—who would become better known by her stage name Peggy—seems to have suffered from slight lapses of memory, and there were holes galore in the tales she related in an interview conducted during the 1950s (some of which were mentioned in Charles Foster's book). One claim was that she was Arthur's natural daughter, another that she was born in 1904—and this year appears in her *IMDb* (*Internet Movie Database*) profile, although the actual date of April 22 may well be correct.

But the census confirms that when she was only a matter of months old, in June 1900, Arthur had already been dead over two years. And, as for 1904, well that was the year of the St. Louis Olympics, but Marjorie was actually born in the year when the Games of the II Olympiad were held in Paris.

Further proof comes in the 1900 census, which shows—albeit as an apparent afterthought if you see the original return—that Marie was Frank Prevost's step-daughter, whereas Marjorie was clearly described as Frank's "daughter."

Also included within the census are details of the place of birth of the various individuals, and also of each person's parents. Frank Prevost's mother and father were both born in Switzerland, and a nickname for Ouray City is . . . the "Switzerland of America."

Well I thought it was interesting.

So, we have reached the start of the twentieth century and the very short life of the infant Marie Prevost has been far from uneventful.

Unraveling contradictory evidence spanning just a handful of years has already proved problematic—a theme I fear will continue.

SINFUL PRIDE, ENORMOUS GUILT

During the early part of the 1900s, the Prevost family left Colorado for Los Angeles. Before 1920—and almost certainly before 1915—Frank and Hughina went their separate ways, although Hughina and her daughters retained the family name.

The chances of discovering much about Marie's teenage years are, at best, slim; Marie herself was believed to have said she had enjoyed a privileged upbringing and was educated at the finest schools. The former surely cannot be true—losing your father in such awful circumstances does not (in my opinion at least) come under the general heading of "privileged," so it seems reasonable to suppose that the school(s) Marie attended were not of the quality she had suggested.

But there was a reason behind the apparent need to exaggerate, or completely reinvent the truth, and that need arose when Marie became one of Hollywood director Mack Sennett's "Bathing Beauties." According to one source, she had been "discovered" after supposedly delivering some legal papers to the studio (for she was a clerk in a law firm . . . apparently), before being persuaded to be a background extra in a short film.

The Canadian Sennett, birth name Michael Sinnott, was the founder of Keystone Studios and the creator of what became known as slapstick comedy. As the popularity of his bumbling policemen, the "Keystone Cops," began to wane, Sennett introduced a number of beautiful young girls, provocatively (under-)dressed, who would feature in comedy shorts or various promotional activities.

According to Brent Walker's book *Mack Sennett's Fun Factory*, Sennett was "inspired" (if that's the right word) by a front-page newspaper photo of a pretty young girl who had been involved in a traffic accident. It seems that the display of bare knees was as newsworthy as the incident itself: "Go hire some girls, any girls, so long as they're pretty. Especially around the knees."

Or so goes Sennett's version of the birth of the Bathing Beauties.

In 1923, Marie told *Motion Picture World* that Sennett had looked stern as she entered his office—so much so that Marie was almost reduced to tears. But Sennett's expression suddenly changed, and a smile spread across his face: "'I want your signature today,' he said. 'Sign right there.' I suddenly realized the paper he pushed in front of me was a contract. I was to be one of Sennett's Bathing Beauties. Best of all I was to be paid $15 a week. I signed without reading a word. Fifteen dollars was a lot of money."

Pictures and the Picturegoer in November 1924, reckoned that Sennett had been impressed by Marie's face and "fine carriage," as well as her "impudence and freshness." The article claimed that Sennett soon discovered that Marie wasn't just pretty she was also an excellent swimmer, and the producer was impressed enough to apparently hire the teenager there and then.

The girls were pictured with Sennett's comedians: the response was positive. The next step was logical enough: "Get those kids on the screen. Sure I know they can't act, but they don't have to act. Put them in bathing suits and just have them around to be looked at while the comics are making funny."

Chauvinistic—but it made money.

In actual fact, some of the "kids" most certainly could act, and Marie Prevost was by no means the only girl to make the transition from bathing costume to recognized performer—Phyllis Haver and (albeit much later) Carole Lombard are both worthy of mention.

Marie's "missing" two years are now more readily explained, as youth was very much a prerequisite for Bathing Beauty status—the "beauty" being vital by definition. Sennett himself was more than capable of exaggeration when it came to revealing the pasts of some of his girls, but another reason for hiding the truth would surely have been due to the morality of the era.

Having a divorcée for a mother—notwithstanding what had befallen Arthur Dunn—was not great for the reputation of studio or aspiring starlet, and neither was the fact that she had a half-sister and not one of the "full" variety.

What shocked me was the sheer extent of the lies that were told to protect an individual or corporate image.

As Marie's popularity began to grow, the name of Frank Prevost was simply erased from existence—to the extent that researchers wondered whether he had actually died, rather than being estranged from Hughina. (For the record, Frank was living in what was almost certainly a boarding house in Precinct Fifty-Seven in San Diego Township when the 1920 census was taken, and his marital status was indeed given as "divorced".)

Frank was "replaced" by a bank manager named Eric Prevost, who had supposedly died unexpectedly, right around the time when Marie started working for Sennett—the need to work to support her "widowed" mother would have been far more socially acceptable than the reality of the situation.

But what of Frank?

He must have been aware about what was being said, yet seemingly he never spoke—at least publicly—about the separation from his wife, the identity of his step-daughter, and the apparent creation of the fictional Eric (who Peggy described as a "wonderful man!").

If Frank did indeed carry the deception to his grave, he kept quiet for a good few years—he passed away sometime around September 1933.

For his part, Sennett seemed happy to be involved in the charade. He stated—via studio releases, which obviously need to be taken with the proverbial pinch of salt—that Marie's background was "Anglo-Irish," "French-Canadian," and "Scottish-English"; her "father," the ever-mysterious Eric, was "an amateur athlete of word class" and even an international skier. For her part, Marie—according to the *Pictures and the Picturegoer* piece from November 1924—"used to wrap up in furs and tam-o'-shanter and tramp out in the Canadian snows, where she would sport a toboggan and pair of skis with the best man of them all."

Hughina was no longer the recently-divorced former widow of a railroad worker: she was an ex-ballerina, from whom Marie had inherited her grace and poise. When she had hung up her ballet shoes, she became an astute and high-powered business executive, and Marie's education in a Montreal convent had left her fluent in French.

Sennett hailed from Quebec and any French phrases that Marie may have been able to drop into conversations or interviews had presumably been taught by Sennett—and not a nun. Marie had probably never even been to Montreal, but according to Sennett, she was a champion swimmer who still held "a number of diving records."

(Other schools I've seen mentioned include Laurette Sisters' School in Denver and St Mary's in Los Angeles—maybe she went to one, or both . . . or neither.)

Sublime-to-ridiculous time now, as it was also claimed that Marie's Scottish heritage meant she was one of a very select few who could prepare "the Highland delicacy, haggis!"

Doubtless whilst reciting the recipe in French, before completing a perfect dive with a forward double somersault—pike position.

Incroyable!

Earlier, I mentioned an appearance as an extra in one of Mack Sennett's short films. Initially, it seemed that the movie in question could have been a 1915 work entitled *Those Bitter Sweets*, a twelve minute one-reeler starring the Australian-born, future Laurel-and-Hardy stalwart Mae Busch. The short still exists. I've watched it, and I've absolutely no idea at all if Marie Prevost is in the film. Part of *Those Bitter Sweets* is set in what appears to be an ice cream parlor; there are a couple of girls in the scene, one of whom might just be Marie, but I'm consoled—to an extent, anyway—by the fact that better people than me don't know for sure.

Because Sennett's Bathing Beauties were included in his short films purely to please the eye, their appearances were rarely credited, so there has to be an element of reliance on movie records for some sort of confirmation regarding films in which Marie may or may not have featured. When I first started compiling this book, Marie was listed by *IMDb* as an uncredited extra in *Those Bitter Sweets*. By proofreading time, her name had been removed. Cue a bit of a rewrite. . . .

So, according to—and assuming the accuracy of—*IMDb*, Marie's filmography totals an impressive 120, although within the list are a string of shorts, unconfirmed or uncredited parts, and minor roles. The plan is to mention the films in passing, but concentrate on just a few as we meander through Marie's professional and private life.

To give some indication as to how prolific the Sennett studios were, in excess of 100 titles were released during 1915: Marie

Prevost appeared in but one—probably—entitled *His Father's Footsteps,* which was released on November 28.

According to the *Silent Era* web site, the survival status of this two-reel film is "unknown"—I'd venture so far as to say "gone for good."

Four more titles followed in 1916: *Better Late than Never, Unto Those Who Sin, Sunshine,* and *A Scoundrel's Toll.* The first-named film starred Mae Busch—again—the second was the first time Marie's role was credited. She played Celeste, thereby affording me a golden opportunity for some sort of "Marie Celeste" joke, which I am going to graciously decline.

Sunshine also featured Gloria Swanson and a fellow Bathing Beauty (and one of Marie's closest friends), Phyllis Haver.

There was a trio of appearances in 1917: *Her Nature Dance, Secrets of a Beauty Parlor,* and *Two Crooks.* But of far more interest, because I have far more information. . . .

Mack Sennett's bathing girls regularly participated in local pageants and what were effectively beauty contests. At the 1917 Great Bathing Parade, held in Venice, California (on June 10), Bathing Beauties pretty much swept the board. The competition winner was Mary Thurman, Jaunita Hansen was the runner-up, and joint third were Marie Prevost and Maude Wayne.

If you thought the Great Bathing Parade was just a small event to which Sennett's finest just had to turn up to be assured of recognition, then you'd be wrong. This is from the June 25, 1917, issue of *Mack Sennett Weekly*: "If pride be sinful, then our guilt is enormous. We are unable to contemplate the honors and prizes won by the Mack Sennett-Keystone girls at the annual Venice bathing suit parade without visibly swelling. It was a wonderful tribute to the charm and beauty of the Sennett-Keystone girls."

I suppose that the source of the article gave a fair indication as to the bias of what followed, for example: "From a field of scores of pretty girls who competed for the prizes, the Sennett-Keystone girls swept off nearly all the honors. All that was left for the other lesser beauties was a lungful of ocean breeze."

There was a bit of background to what was clearly a very significant event. This particular Venice was situated less than twenty miles from Los Angeles, and it had been built in the style of its illustrious Italian namesake, with houses situated next to a string of canals. The contest grew from a simple wager between two gentlemen into a spectacular competition to determine which young lady looked the best in a bathing suit.

Hyperbole notwithstanding, the fact that 75,000 people came to watch the parade of beauties parading along a long wooden stage—specially erected for the contest—is genuinely impressive. 1917 was the official debut of the girls from the Sennett studio and they were in competition with "the flower of screen pulchritude—the selected beauties of the different studios."

Other girls had the apparent benefit of young men with megaphones practically begging the crowds to cheer for their studio favorites, but without even the merest hint of impartiality or exaggeration, Sennett's magazine declared that no encouragement was needed for its own studio's girls—in fact the whole 75,000 strong crowd apparently cheered wildly every time the name of a Sennett-Keystone beauty was announced.

Despite winning prizes galore, the reporter was keen to show that the girls' qualities extended beyond their physical attributes: "Most of the girls from this [*Sennett's*] studio have been recruited from schools and colleges. Nearly all of them live at home with their families in Los Angeles. They are all sweet, and young, and wholesome. Gloriously young and gloriously healthy and genuine."

Just in case you were wondering, Marie wore an orange and black shepherdess costume with appropriate hat and staff, supplied by the Bernal Dyas Company of Los Angeles. And I *loved* this comment, also taken from the magazine: "When Marie Prevost went onto the platform to get third prize she was so bewildered by the battery of cameras that she tried to smile at all of them and spun round and round until she was dizzy."

Nearly ready to head into 1918 now. Quite a few movies lay in prospect for Marie Prevost, as well as—and whisper it quietly—a secret marriage. But before this chapter closes, there's just time for a first dip into my limited collection of memorabilia: an original 1923 press photo of Marie Prevost, the Bathing Beauty.

GERKE THE JERKY

Marie appeared in ten pictures during 1918: *His Hidden Purpose, Those Athletic Girls, Friend Husband* (which I initially misread as Fried Husband), *His Smothered Love, Her Screen Idol, She Loved Him Plenty, Sleuths, Whose Little Wife are You?, Hide and Seek, Detectives,* and *The Village Chestnut*.

Ben Turpin starred in three of the films. The famously cross-eyed Turpin claimed his right eye was knocked out of alignment due to an accident whilst performing on stage; he reportedly insured his eyes with Lloyd's of London in case they became "uncrossed!"

Phyllis Haver featured in five of the films and another "regular" was a lightly marked brindle Great Dane called Teddy—also known as "Keystone Teddy," "Teddy the Wonder Dog," or the less flattering "Sennett Dog." So popular was the dog, that his "salary" was rumored to be $350 a week—which I am (un)reliably informed equates to nearly $6,000 in today's money (something approaching £4,000 sterling). Now that's quite a few bones.

But the early part of this chapter is more concerned with Marie's secret marriage—a relationship that remained hidden from all but a very select few. Although sources differ (some will quote 1919), I am using June 22, 1918, as the date when Marie tied the knot with a socialite named H.C. (Henry Charles) "Sonny" (sometimes "Sunny") Gerke, whose profession—depending on who you believe—was either an "automobile dealer" or a "seaman."

According to the 1920 census, Marie was living with her mother and sister in Los Angeles. Described as single (she wasn't) and nineteen years of age (she certainly wasn't), there is no mention of Sonny Gerke.

Mack Sennett was one of those who knew the truth, as he recounted (salt at the ready) in his memoirs: "It was 1919. 'My husband has left me,' she [*Marie*] said. 'Husband?' I said. 'How can you have a husband. You aren't even married.' 'Yes I am,' she said. 'I've been married six months and we haven't even had a honeymoon. Now he's left me.'"

The "he" was Sonny Gerke, and it seems that the couple had wed one night after a party. Reading extracts from *Stardust and Shadows* and all the available quotes—and assuming they have some basis in fact—the Gerke-Prevost union was pretty well doomed from the outset. Marie allegedly told her sister that straight after the wedding, her new husband had gone home by himself because his mother was expecting him!

Gerke promised Marie that he would tell his mother about his new actress bride—but he didn't.

Maybe Gerke felt unable to tell his mother that his wife was a Bathing Beauty, or perhaps he was simply too much of a mummy's boy and wasn't brave enough to come clean and face what presumably would have been his mother's wrath?

Whatever the case, although Marie apparently did visit the Gerke mansion, her "occupation" was never discussed. This led to the ridiculous situation of Mrs. Gerke reputedly seeing Marie "arrested"—but totally failing to see the camera and film crew behind a nearby truck. She duly told Sonny that Marie was not the sort of person she wanted in her son's life, and the dutiful Sonny rang Marie to tell her that their sham of a marriage was over.

A distinction needs to be made between "verbally over" and "officially over;" Gerke was unwilling to divorce on the basis that his mother didn't know he was even married, and as Marie's career and popularity were on the rise, she didn't want the negative publicity that news of a divorce case might bring.

In fact, it wasn't until the latter half of 1923 when events necessitated that the couple legally divorce. (Marie was in a new relationship and wanted to marry.)

On August 23, 1923, this notice appeared in *Time Magazine*: "Sued for divorce. Mrs. Marie Gerke (Marie Prevost), cinema actress, by H. C. Gerke, automobile salesman, in Los Angeles. He charged desertion. She was generally believed to be unmarried until the divorce suit was filed."

The divorce was finalized on October 7, 1924, by which time Marie was already engaged—but that's for a later chapter. This little snippet was found in a paper called *New Zealand Truth*: "We were just two foolish children who ran away, married and separated immediately. (The marriage was kept secret five years before divorce was asked. Gerke was a sailor when he met Marie at a house party at Oceanside, California, and married her.)"

The *Los Angeles Times* edition from August 12, 1923, confirmed that: "closest friends have long been kept in the dark" about Marie's marriage. This was echoed by Mack Sennett in 1954, when he suggested that he, Marie, and the two witnesses at the ceremony knew of the union, although "I suppose Gerke the Jerky must have had some idea too," he added.

"I always called him Gerke the Jerky; he must have been to leave a lovely girl like Marie."

Marrying young, before fame came knocking, was far from unusual—I have also written about Jean Harlow and Marilyn Monroe, and Messrs. McGrew and Dougherty were their respective first (and swiftly discarded) husbands. The subject of short-lived, almost clandestine unions was discussed thus in *Picture-Play* magazine during 1931:

> I think Marie Prevost started all this in 1918 when she secretly married H. C. Gerke, a seaman, and the custom has continued without interruption until now. Quite a few stars have had husbands almost in hiding. Miss Prevost met young Gerke at a house party, fell hard for the naval lad, and under the spell of a June moon and a romantic night rushed off to find a justice of the peace....
>
> They were divorced in 1923—friendly and companionable. Members of the film colony who often saw the two together, believed young Gerke to be just an admirer. He passed out of Marie's life, a man of mystery.

Even if they parted on amicable terms, there has been little to suggest that there was any great depth of feeling between Marie and Sonny Gerke. However, in a *Motion Picture* feature printed several years later, Marie revealed her thoughts on that old four-letter word—"love"—and the young man who first captured her heart.

She had met the person concerned whilst swimming—he was on a yacht and invited Marie aboard. She explained: "His name was Gerke, but we called him Sunny. He was twenty-two and Castilian-Spanish. He was like a dream come true. The whole thing was like a dream—for that matter."

The idea of marriage appears to have been Sunny/Sonny's—but the thought clearly excited Marie. She had always lived with her mother and apparently hadn't really been allowed to go out very often—and when she did, her mother would always be waiting for her to come home. To Marie, marriage equaled freedom, and the transition from being a girl to a woman.

However, Marie's immaturity led her to believe that getting married so young meant that she and Sunny shared a big secret. Marie revealed she had loved secrets ever since she had been a small child: "We slipped off to Oceanside and were married. We didn't tell anyone. For three years not a soul knew we were married. Even Phyllis Haver, my best friend, was never certain."

Marie claimed that the relationship lasted eight months—during which she described walking "on clouds of happiness." That seems to fly in the face of earlier comments Marie had made about their relationship—or rather lack of it. This article was printed soon after the breakdown of her second marriage. Perhaps her memories of Gerke—the innocence, romance and excitement of the whole situation—affected Marie in some way: "At first it was truly thrilling.... [*but*] I don't know what happened to break the illusion. Nothing specific. Just what it is that turns clouds from beautiful, fluffy billows to dark threatening storm-containers? But suddenly the dream was over."

Well, this is all very different to other accounts I've read, but worse than the knowledge that her feelings had subsided was Marie's realization of the lengths to which she had gone to hide the truth: "I had lied about my age. I had lied to my mother. I had lied to my friends. My life [*was*] a bunch of lies entangling me like the threads of a spider web enmeshing a fly."

She claimed that her husband wanted to tell everybody about the couple's marriage, describing his wish as "man-like," which is about as far removed as you can get from Foster's text. The truth? Well I suppose you could always decide on the toss of a coin, but I'd hazard a guess that the reality lies somewhere a little closer to Foster's theory than Marie's prosaic words.

Although her private life may have been far from perfect during 1918 and 1919, Marie Prevost was much in demand professionally.

1919 was a prolific year in front of the camera, but her athletic five-feet-four-inch frame, dark brown hair, and big blue eyes were attracting the attention of others apart from Sonny Gerke. Marie was starting to receive significant amounts of fan mail; some addressed by way of a description, so rarely were Sennett's girls credited on screen. The hugely influential newspaper publisher William Randolph Hearst was in the process of recruiting performers for his new project, *Cosmopolitan Productions*. Marie was on Hearst's wanted list, and he was prepared to pay a lot of money to secure her services—$750 per week. Marie told *Photoplay* that "it seemed like a fortune"—it was . . . more than double the going rate for a dog in fact.

Marie's assessment of the offer was both objective and mature. Her films to date had been relatively short two-reelers, and now she was being considered for five- and six-reel movies. Marie said she "wasn't stupid enough to think I was as good an actress as the others he [Hearst] had hired so I went to Mr. Sennett and asked for his advice."

Sennett told Marie that whilst he was willing to release her from her contract, he felt she would benefit from waiting and gaining more experience, and he would be raising her salary to $250 per week with immediate effect. All of which suggests Marie was a very level-headed and loyal young woman—good qualities to have.

Although her "reward" was only one-third of the wage she could have earned, her increased salary certainly compared favorably with others on Mack Sennett's payroll. Gloria Swanson was earning $65 a week at the time—according to Sennett's records—Phyllis Haver $125, and Charlie Chaplin (pre-tramp) $185.

Whilst still under the Keystone wing, Marie's 1919 offerings comprised: *Never Too Old* (which featured the instantly recognizable James Finlayson—double-take and fade master in a very early role), *Rip & Stitch: Tailors*, and *East Lynne with Variations*. The latter featured Marie as the heroine of an apparently excellent comic spoof in which she faced one dramatic ordeal after another, only to be saved by the dashing hero Ben Turpin—actually forget the "dashing."

A *Photoplay* review described Marie as "exquisite," before adding: "Ben Turpin is the hero. Whose heart is true though his eyes are not"!

The list continued with *Yankee Doodle in Berlin* (aka *The Kaiser's Last Squeal*), which starred well-known female impersonator Bothwell Browne as Captain Bob White, who spent most of the film in drag—good casting then. Despite its theme, the film's release was delayed until a few months after the armistice was signed, which brought the First World War to an end.

Sennett gave Marie the lead in the five-reeler. With the money on the table from *Cosmopolitan*, Sennett must have been aware that Marie's days as a Bathing Beauty were numbered, but he was still prepared to place her in the spotlight, as it were. He wasn't as willing to match the pay offer, though—I've read a quote stating "start with Sennett, get rich somewhere else."

"All the Sennett girls appeared in the first part," noted Wesley Driscoll of *Photoplay*, "but only Marie Prevost had anything to do with the story proper." The movie was a box office hit and, in part, must have paved the way for Marie's eventual departure to *Universal* Studios (in 1921). "A lot of the fun had gone. . . ." Marie told *Photoplay*. "Everything was ruled by money."

Then came *Reilly's Wash Day, Why Beaches Are Popular, Love's False Faces, The Dentist,* and *Uncle Tom Without a Cabin*. The names Conklin, Turpin, Finlayson, and Haver still feature heavily, and they all appeared in one or more of the last trio of Marie's 1919 films: *Up in Alf's Place, Salome vs. Shenandoah,* and *The Speakeasy*. The last of those films elicited these fairly damning comments in *Photoplay*: "Mack Sennett people are, more and more, deliberately setting out to be funny. For some months now, the output . . . has been inclined to be heavy, dull, and ponderous. The director works too hard; the sub-title writer tries too desperately to be funny."

Although the reviewer did concede that Marie: "is beautiful in a bathing suit"—shame the film wasn't set at the seaside then.

Marie wasn't as busy on screen in 1920. *A Kitchen Cinderella, Down on the Farm, Fresh From the City, You Wouldn't Believe It, His Youthful Fancy, Movie Fans,* and *Love, Honor and Behave!* are the films listed on the *IMDb* site, but it seemed that Sennett's offerings had found some favor amongst the critics. One review of *Love, Honor and Behave!* reckoned that the film "points a moral and adorns a tale with the aid of slapstick and hokum"—whatever that means—and that "Sennett approaches his high-watermark here. It is a return to his old satisfying standards."

In 1921, however, Marie would make a further half a dozen pictures for Sennett before heading for pastures new: the six were *Dabbling in Art*, *On a Summer Day*, *A Small Town Idol*, *Wedding Bells Out of Tune*, *She Sighed by the Seaside*, and *Call a Cop*.

The termination of her Sennett contract was by mutual consent, although very much at Marie's instigation. It was related that two long-term contract offers were made in the fortnight after her split from Sennett, but as Marie signed a reported three-year contract with Universal Studios, it seemed that she was genuinely grateful for the start Mack Sennett had given her: "I am glad to be out of comedy, but just the same I wouldn't take a million dollars for the training I had. It gives you the sureness and technique that nothing else can give you."

The following extract is taken from the July 1921 issue of *Photoplay*, and afterwards, I think I might just take a little time to dwell on one or two of the comments made in Joan Jordan's piece of incredibly flowery prose—and bear in mind that Marie hadn't really appeared in any films of note at this point:

> *She is the product of ultra-sophistication. She is the embodiment of the 20th century—the incarnation of Paris after the war. Her simplicity is the simplicity of the 'petit Trianon'. Her worldly wisdom has been absorbed through the tips of fingers, in the air she breathed, the very thoughts the world is thinking. . . .*
>
> *She might be fourteen—eighteen—twenty. Her extreme youth holds all the intriguing promises of immaturity. Her appeal is suggestion. Yet neither the freshness of her cheek nor the firmness of her flesh hide the open secret that her youth is the youth of the city pavements and white lights. . . .*

Or in other words, she's an attractive young woman who could become a half-decent actress.

For the record, le Petit Trianon is a small château, which is situated in the grounds of the Palace de Versailles in France. Seemingly, the construction was notable for a move towards a more refined style of architecture. Marie had already been described as ultra-sophisticated, "refined" means pretty much the same thing, so Ms. Jordan did something I'm sure only a woman could get away with and complimented a fellow female by comparing her to a house.

I'm also a bit unsure about the "fourteen—eighteen—twenty" paragraph. Notwithstanding the fact that Marie was actually twenty-four at the time and very much a grown woman, was it just indicative of the time that someone barely in their teens could have some sort of suggestive appeal based around a lack of maturity? Whilst I would concede that youth may have had benefits in the silent film industry, where was the cut-off point? Lucille Ricksen was of the right age to have this "appeal," yet before her untimely death, she was being passed off as *older* than her tender years. Confusing.

Anyway, the article continued to say that Marie had real comedy instinct because she was able to be funny without actually looking funny. And, in all probability, Marie possessed dramatic talents that could "make you laugh with a lump in your throat and smile with tears on your cheeks." If the author was correct in her assumptions, Marie would apparently be able to "take the earth in her hand and juggle it any way she pleased." Apparently....

There then followed a little more insight into Marie herself, her personality, and appearance. She revealed that it took very little to make her cry. If anything, even if not remotely, serious happened to a child, an elderly person, or an animal, tears would invariably be shed and, she continued: "it's strange—but little things, hurts, humiliations, baby tears, always seem to affect me most."

Marie was described as having blue-black hair with a soft wave, and her sparkling "gray-blue" eyes were sometimes all blue sometimes all gray and sometimes a bit green with a "very, very merry" expression—I have no idea how eyes can do all that. Her skin was white, instead of creamy, and her mouth was described a "little" [*which is fine*], "red" [*so is that*] and "pathetic" [*is that a compliment?!*]. Marie would use her hands when she talked with the "abandon of a Frenchwoman," a "freedom from self-consciousness" inherited from her French ancestry—for she was "French-Canadian, with a dash—a very big dash—of Irish."

The one personal disappointment at the end of this occasionally fascinating piece is that I'm now far too old to try to flatter a young lady, 1920s style: "Well hi! I love the way your eyes keep changing color. Your mouth is simply pathetic and you look like a building: will you go on a date with me?!"

Marie's first movie for Universal was entitled *Moonlight Follies*—"Marie is certainly good for the eyes, and it is well to rest the brain occasionally," was *Photoplay*'s assessment. The prolific and successful, yet tragically ill-fated, future *MGM* producer Irving Thalberg decided he wanted to promote Marie's inaugural performance for her new employer. He took her to the company's summer meeting in Chicago, where he announced her appearance in *The Butterfly* (which would later be renamed *Moonlight Follies*) and then she was dispatched to New York's Coney Island, where a large number of onlookers watched a very public burning of her trademark bathing suit—described as a "lacrimose rite" in *Motion Picture* magazine—to symbolize the end of her time as a Mack Sennett ingénue.

More "publicity" was gained with the reporting of a story concerning dramatic events in a swimming pool, during filming in July 1921. According to Sally Dumaux, in her book *King Baggot: A Biography and Filmography of the First King of the Movies*, the film's director, William "King" Baggot, and his assistant Nat Ross supposedly got into difficulty before Marie came to the rescue.

Ross, described as a "splendid swimmer," suffered a reaction to diving into the cold pool and Baggot, himself a "powerful swimmer," slipped on wet concrete as he went to Ross's aid and knocked himself out.

Cue the ex-Bathing Beauty who dragged Ross from the water, whilst Baggot came round and was able to get out of the pool unaided, but presumably groggy.

Part of me now feels guilty that I doubted the ever-doubtable Mack Sennett when he described Marie as a "champion swimmer."

Anyway, back to *Moonlight Follies*. In the film, Marie plays Nan Rutledge, who performs dances to attract male attention, but her father insists that she finds herself a "decent" husband. Nan picks on George Fillmore, a man she presumes will want nothing to do with her; to her surprise, he eventually proposes—but she turns him down.

George takes the rejection well and promptly abducts Nan, and whilst in a secluded mountain hideaway, the couple fall in love—as you do.

The critic Grace Kingsley, writing in the *Los Angeles Times*, considered that Marie was going to become "a screen favorite—even clothed and away from her professional bathing suit." The onscreen move from partially to fully clad allowed audiences and critics alike to focus on Marie's acting skills, rather than her physical attributes. In Grace Kingsley's opinion, Marie possessed: "an expressive face and a vivid and arresting screen personality . . . in addition to which she shows evidence of developing into a brilliant screen comedienne."

The King-Prevost partnership was quickly reunited in a comedy entitled *Nobody's Fool*, and Marie Prevost's breakthrough year ended with *A Parisian Scandal*—a film that also featured Mae Busch.

Before we trundle into 1922, is it possible to form any early opinions of the aspiring young actress?

Well, even though she wouldn't have remembered her father, the loss of a parent must have had some sort of an impact—maybe more on her mother or the family unit in general. There is nothing to suggest that Hughina would have moved at all—let alone to the United States—had Arthur not lost his life, and I suppose you can draw your own conclusion as to whether the journey south was an upheaval or an adventure for young Marie.

Her impetuous, almost reckless, decision to marry Sonny Gerke might indicate an understandable emotional naivety, although her husband was not really of an age (or maturity) to be seen as a replacement father figure. Keeping the relationship—such as it was—secret, was probably a sensible career move, although the revelation of secrets was one of the prices of fame that Marie paid after her marriage had taken place.

As a Bathing Beauty and aspiring starlet, Marie seemed very self-aware. If she thought she had ability, she realized it needed to be nurtured, and that experience with Sennett was initially worth more than the lure of the proverbial fast buck. Yet, when Marie felt the time was right to develop herself as an actress—which effectively meant a move away from Mack Sennett—Marie seemed to have been assured enough to resolve a potentially awkward situation herself.

The admission that it took little to make her cry is actually quite endearing—and that word probably best describes the impression I have formed, so far, of this talented, undeniably pretty young woman: endearing, but with maybe just a hint of fragility or vulnerability.

THE FLAPPER

The term "flapper" first appeared after the end of the First World War: in Britain, it meant young, perhaps slightly awkward girls, but in America the definition of the word had more rebellious undertones. With the First World War at an end, the 1920s witnessed a definite shift in attitudes amongst the younger generation, and out of this was born the flapper.

Fashion and hairstyles started to change—skirts became shorter, underwear less restrictive, stockings would be worn, make-up became far more popular, and longer hair was replaced by the short bob.

The flapper was brash, blunt, and overtly sexy; they smoked and—despite Prohibition—openly drank alcohol. They partied and danced—the fast pace of the dances matching their wild lifestyles. The recklessness of the decade would be brought to an abrupt end by the Wall Street Crash of 1929, but, up until that point, the 1920s had been a time of change—and the age of the flapper.

Marie, in a striped bathing suit and bizarrely holding what looks like a goose on a lead, graced the front cover of the first issue of *The Flapper* magazine in May 1922. This was the question posed to readers on the new monthly that cost "two dimes a copy" or "two bucks a year": "How do you like our girl on the cover? Some fascinating little minx, Marie Prevost, isn't she? And who but she could assume such a fascinating pose?"

A competition followed. All the reader had to do was describe, in less than fifty words, their opinion of what was suggested by the picture, with a prize of $5 being up for grabs for the winner. The next twenty-four best entries would receive a signed photograph of Marie—personally I'd have preferred the signed photo, but I guess my attempt would have arrived over ninety years too late....

Anyway, back to the start of 1922, and the picture on the previous page is a scanned image from the January 1922 issue of *Screenland*. The photograph was taken by Edwin Bower Hesser (1893-1962), who is probably best known for a collection of risqué shots of Jean Harlow taken in Griffith Park, Los Angeles, around 1929.

Marie's new-found status seemingly entitled her to named parts in movies, as opposed to the numerous uncredited Bathing Beauty appearances. First of all, she played Patricia Parker in *Don't Get Personal*, followed by Teddy Harmon in *The Dangerous Little Demon*. Of the former, *The Film Daily* commented:

> Once more the former Sennett bathing beauty succeeds in holding the attention (or is it the eye?) in a picture that without her would certainly be dull. She is beautifully photographed, wears some charming frocks and besides there is a certain atmosphere that puts her in a class with Gloria Swanson and a very few others who possess a greater degree of feminine appeal than the average actress.

Those two movies were released in January and March respectively, but in the intervening period—on February 15, to be exact—Marie was quoted in the *San Francisco Call* in the aftermath of the murder (on February 1) of the director William Desmond Taylor. From what I have read, no firm evidence has ever been found to confirm the identity of Taylor's killer.

An actress named Margaret Gibson gave a deathbed "confession" in 1964, and another suspect was Mary Miles Minter, who was mentioned in the *San Francisco Call* article. She was an actress nearly thirty years Taylor's junior.

Copies of passionate love letters sent to Taylor shattered Minter's wholesome screen image, and she was vilified in the press. Some believe that Taylor did not share Minter's feelings, but whatever the truth, Mary Miles Minter would leave the film industry for good in 1923.

The article started with Marie's response to what was described as a "chorus of protests" against the perception of Hollywood excess. Marie claimed that it was wrong for the public to be so ready to believe any and every bit of gossip involving a well-known name from the movie industry, and that "the suggestions of scandal, of dope and riotous living are doing incalculable damage to the industry."

Marie then maintained that "the people at Hollywood are hard working and there isn't much time for carousal." All those involved with making films would be on set at half past eight every morning, working all day, every day, and often into the night and, according to Marie, it simply wasn't possible to live a life of constant excess and still turn up promptly on set the following morning.

As far as the inference of drug taking was concerned, Marie stated that she had never used dope—moreover she didn't know anyone in Hollywood who took drugs: "That's all a fairy tale," she asserted. The reality may have deviated slightly from Marie's outwardly naïve perspective, but she went on to argue that it was impossible for an actress to be a drug user and keep her looks: "Just think how dissipation would show in her face in the close-ups on the screen!"

The reporter's logical follow-up question was how movie stars spent their spare time if they weren't enjoying the high life. Marie's rather unexpected reply was that she watched as many films as she could in order to study the performances of other actresses. The public at large simply did not realize just how studious, how "normal" many actresses actually were. Mabel Normand was cited as an example—she was often surrounded by books, and Marie couldn't recall ever seeing Mary Miles Minter without her mother. The article concluded with Marie flat-batting the reference to the ongoing murder mystery: "She said she had known Taylor, like everybody else at Hollywood, that he was a 'nice man' and 'a great favorite with the players.'"

Intriguingly, Mabel Normand—who herself died in 1930—was the last-known person to see William Desmond Taylor alive; she had visited him on the evening of his death. In contrast to Marie's comments about drugs, Mabel Normand was hooked on cocaine. Taylor was believed to have met with attorneys with a view to pressing charges against her suppliers. Normand was ruled out as a suspect, but believed Taylor's involvement in her drug addiction may have been a reason for his murder.

Interesting article though, especially Marie's views—albeit they're more likely to be "Universal" rather than purely personal—on Hollywood excesses. Is it possible that Marie buried herself so deeply in her work that she effectively sheltered herself from the parties and drugs to which many in the movie industry were regularly exposed?

Like most things about Marie Prevost, we will never know for certain, but from all the newspaper articles I've found, none suggest that Marie's flapper image was genuinely representative of the person away from the cameras.

Early in 1922, Marie reflected on her change of studio—and career direction:

> *I want to be something, not just look something.* We [Sennett's Bathing girls] *just played around and had a good time except when we stopped to realize we weren't getting anywhere. That is I wasn't. I've got all I can get out of it* [this could refer to the wearing a bathing suit, or making comedies], *and now I want to grow. I'm afraid if I stayed on the same line for another year, I should have lost even that inclination. And a bathing girl doesn't have very much time.*

Marie's next film was *The Crossroads of New York* (for Mack Sennett), followed by the Universal, King Baggot-directed, romantic comedy *Kissed*. In the film, Marie played Constance Keener, who was engaged to the incredibly rich but seemingly unromantic Merton Torrey (J. Frank Glendon). Constance attended a masquerade ball minus her partner, and while she was alone on a balcony, a masked guest grabbed her and kissed her so intensely that she decided he was the man for her.

Unfortunately, but sort of necessarily for the plot, there were two guests in identical costumes; Constance finally chose Dr Sherman Moss (Lloyd Whitlock) and the pair eloped—but during a train journey, Moss kissed Constance and she realized that she was running away with the wrong man.

The train came to a halt and was "held up" by a masked stranger who kissed Constance—ahhh *he* was the one she was supposed to run off with. The mask was removed, the unromantic Torrey was revealed as the best kisser in town, and they all lived etc. etc.

Fairly obvious, but nice plot nonetheless, and the *Motion Picture* review seemed to agree: "A slight little, bright little play ... which carries for its assets, Marie Prevost's piquant personality, which she asserts in a flapperish type of role, a faint dash of romance and some breezy titles wholly in keeping with the fabric of the plot."

Another critic clearly enjoyed the picture, but expressed his regret at not being one of the men with whom Marie exchanged what he described as "osculatory offerings" with the "dainty little star!"

Apparently there were scenes in *Kissed* that involved a number of babies: "They're pretty good," Marie revealed, "but King Baggot and I have to take two hours off every day while the actors and actresses take their naps, But of course when they all start crying at once, we just take to the back lot and wait until the row is over."

Along with the critical reviews and the growing number of interviews in which Marie featured, there were also more light-hearted pieces in fan magazines, which afforded the reader a brief peep into the life of this particular emerging Hollywood star—viz. this extract from the May 1922 issue of *Picture-Play*, which concerned some location filming:

> *My first impression of a bathing beauty was certainly not disillusioning. She looked just like a big doll, really! Her brown hair hung in ringlets all around her face and in curls over her shoulders; she has big, round gray-blue eyes, a regular rosebud mouth, and a cute turned-up nose, and you know how she's built—so perfectly rounded and just a nice size. Marie Prevost is just about the cutest thing I ever saw—except Bebe Daniels.*

I suppose being the second "cutest thing" is still an achievement—and in the lip department, "rosebud" surely beats "pathetic" every time.

Fashion and beauty took up plenty of column inches, and Marie's picture was used to endorse any number of products: "Zip is marvelous for clearing the skin of superfluous hair, says the charming Marie Prevost," and "Liquid Lashlux for long dark lashes" etc. And, during 1922, Marie discussed the reasons why her hair had been cut into a short bob: "For the same reason that most women do most things. Just because I wanted to!"

I'm in no position to pass comment on any hairstyle, but according to Marie, the bob combined beauty, comfort, and time saving, which were deemed to be three reasons that were good enough to do anything. Marie's longer locks had seemingly caused her no end of bother—her hair was naturally curly and "would never stay put" —but the new shorter style was far more practical and manageable. Marie was then quoted as saying: "For a long time my life was just one disappointing, thoroughly defeated bathing cap after another . . . I shall always have one secret sorrow. It is that I didn't have a 'bob' long, long ago."

All of which is fine (albeit slightly surreal), but even if some of the language seems dated, one thing that hasn't changed is the culture of celebrity—in particular the ability of those in the "media" to build up a person with flattering and flowery prose, only to knock them straight back down again. This next—and pretty damning— piece comes from *Motion Picture*: "In my humble opinion, one of the gravest and most expensive mistakes now being made in pictures is the attempt to create a star of the first magnitude out of Marie Prevost."

The reporter conceded that Marie was "a particularly seductive specimen of young womanhood. Not only are her features lovely, but she has the kind of body which sculptors rave over." However, looks alone were no substitute for the "inner qualities" that were required to be a success in Hollywood—qualities that Marie supposedly lacked. And the magazine's view was summed up in just a couple of short sentences: "There was a time when a narrow, almost imperceptible, line divided bathing beauties from dramatic stars. But that line of late has developed into a deep chasm, which no amount of mere loveliness can span."

Back on the big screen, *Her Night of Nights* preceded *The Married Flapper*, in which Marie portrayed Pamela Billings who was a . . . you've guessed haven't you?

The movie itself was described as a "light but entertaining comedy drama," which "holds the interest well, moves along at a snappy pace and for the summer season should prove a welcome attraction in a majority of theaters."

Marie's performance was hailed as a not overly complimentary "entirely adequate," and the leading male role of Bill Billings, which was given to Kenneth Harlan, was considered to be "well cast." More of Mr. Harlan later. . . .

The promotion for the film involved a parade in Kansas during August 1922, where local flappers competed for prizes. The event— as related in *Hollywood Goes Shopping* by David Desser—was featured thus in *Moving Picture World*: "Taking advantage of the park's advertising, the Universal publicity representative ran letters over the signature of Marie Prevost, star in 'The Married Flapper', advising the girls to go and see her in the picture, get pointers then enter the contest."

Apparently, the winner would be invited to the Universal studios for a screen test.

As a slight aside, *The Married Flapper* also showcased the talents of an aspiring young actress named Lucille Ricksen. Actually, when I say "young," I mean "really *really* young."

Although sources vary, I believe Lucille was born on August 22, 1910, and her full name was actually Ingeborg Myrtle Elisabeth Ericksen—the child's mother was also called Ingeborg. Lucille certainly fulfilled the Hollywood prerequisite of being pretty, but what staggered me was not just the tragedy of her death from tuberculosis—although there were rumors of a botched abortion—it was also (in fact more so) that when she passed away on March 13, 1925, Lucille was aged just *fourteen*.

Marie was paired alongside Kenneth Harlan in her next movie, an adaptation of F. Scott Fitzgerald's novel *The Beautiful and Damned*.

By this time, the pair were dating in real life; not only that but both had apparently signed a contract with Warner Brothers. Marie's move to a new studio was being reported widely during July 1922—including the following from *Photoplay*: "Marie Prevost is going to be very dramatic in the future. Her Universal contract having expired, as Universal contracts have a habit of doing, she came to New York, interviewed several producers, and finally decided to be the heroine of the Warner features."

The Beautiful and the Damned was Marie's first released piece of work for the new studio—although it appears to have been the second to be filmed after *Heroes of the Street*—her two-year contract was worth a massive $1,500 per week.

Apparently no copy of *The Beautiful and Damned* exists, but the lobby card, which features Marie as Gloria, includes the caption "Gloria constantly broke engagements—but isn't that the prerogative of the super-flapper?"

As far as the original book's author was concerned, Fitzgerald found it hard to disguise his admiration for the film: ". . . by far the worst movie I've ever seen in my life; cheap, vulgar, ill-constructed and shoddy."

Luckily, audience reaction was far more positive, and in an attempt to raise the profile of the film—and its costars—Jack Warner announced that the couple would marry on the film's set.

Great idea in principle, and if you judge a publicity stunt on popular reaction, then this was a huge success, as literally thousands of fans and well-wishers sent letters and gifts to the couple, and the movie played to packed-out cinemas.

There was only one problem—and it was a big problem.

Marie was still legally married to Sonny Gerke.

The *Los Angeles Mirror* published a story stating that Marie would be committing bigamy if she and Harlan went ahead with the ceremony. Unsurprisingly, Jack Warner was furious—the negative impact on the studio was bad enough, but the "marriage on set" idea had been his, and he must have felt personally slighted by the fact that Marie had not revealed her situation prior to the press article hitting the news-stands.

I've read that Warner arranged an annulment, but I would doubt very much that was actually the case, especially as Marie's divorce from Gerke was factually reported. However, the Prevost-Harlan marriage did eventually take place (in October 1924), well after the furor and scandal had finally died down. Not that Jack Warner ever forgot—as you will soon discover....

The final few words from 1922 come from a *Photoplay* interview conducted by Frederick James Smith: "Shock No.1 occurred at Hotel Biltmore where Miss Prevost was actually ready."

Then, right at the end of the meeting, after Marie had arrived at Muray Studios and changed into a revealing costume, Smith clearly couldn't resist a look: "But the glimpse solved the great international problem. Miss Prevost's vaccination mark is on the left—er—limb, just about six inches north of her knee"

In 1923, Marie appeared alongside Monte Blue in *Brass*—the pair would make eight more movies together over the next two years. *Red Lights*, a *Goldwyn Pictures* murder-mystery—the production company was a forerunner of *MGM*—was her second film of that year, and her final offering was *The Wanters*, a writing credit here for Paul Bern, the second Mr. Jean Harlow, who would take his own life—conspiracy theories notwithstanding—in 1932.

This, by way of a brief digression, is an extract from a biography of the time:

> She [Marie] is under contract with Warner Brothers' organization and will continue playing featured roles in recent "best sellers". She is fast gaining the recognition of the public.
>
> Miss Prevost has never entered stage life, nor has she attempted any other vocation save that of her screen work. She is still a girl of the outdoors. Although golf gets a portion of her spare time, swimming is the more frequent recreation, winter as well as summer.
>
> Her hobbies are dancing and reading.

There was a much longer feature—and therefore a much longer digression—in the March 1923 issue of *Picture-Play*. The interview took place in Marie's Warner Brothers' dressing room and was penned by Constance Palmer.

Marie was wearing a "baby-blue negligee," which, according to the article's author, made her look like a "middle-class schoolgirl who, with tousled head, manicures her fingernails while mother does the dishes."

Emerging from the negligée were legs that were deemed to be "very presentable." Her arms were "round—one with a smudge" and Marie's neck was "very nice." Well that's a relief. This next extract is reproduced verbatim (because I have a copy of the magazine)—the words are Marie's:

> You know I had an awfully cute interview once and the funny part of it was I didn't say a word of it! Everybody asked me how I managed to be so clever, and of course I couldn't think of a thing to tell them. . . .
>
> I suppose lots of actresses wish they could think of literary, epigrammatical things to say on the spur of the moment to writers. Some of 'em study up the night before, but I'd be lost if I hit on a subject the interviewer wanted to discuss.
>
> Most stars feel that way about it, I know. I suppose that's why they ask interviewers to lunch so often. One can always say, 'I like broiled frogs' legs,' and it's sure to create the proper atmosphere on the instant.

> *Right at this minute I'd rather ask you if you think So-and-So's a natural blonde, and if you think a half dozen eggs make as good a shampoo as a dozen. Eggs are so expensive!*
>
> *I can't discuss books with you because, well—I just can't. I read 'em—some of 'em—but I don't talk 'em. But you really should read 'Brass'—it's quite a thing.!* [evidently ironic]
>
> *Seriously though, my part in 'Brass' is the first opportunity I've had to do something a little more—well, a little heavier. I don't aspire to Shakespeare or anything like that, but I have been cast as a frothy-headed flapper ever since I left Sennett's. . . .*

The impression that Ms. Palmer seemed to want to create was that of an assured, yet caring, young woman, who was more relaxed when talking about her friends than herself, and for someone who was emerging from the "veneer of [*Hollywood*] make-believe," Marie seemed wholly unaffected—a trait that the author considered "remarkable." Marie wanted to be liked, but not if it meant changing the person she was.

Parallels were drawn between Marie and Mae Murray, and Marie and Gloria Swanson. Marie may have been deemed by Ms. Palmer to be less mature than the other two actresses—although Gloria Swanson was actually younger—but the trio all had an ability to interact just as easily with teenagers and "oldsters." The article went on to say that: "Motion pictures, part and parcel, are an embodiment of youth—and Marie Prevost is youth sleek and shapely, mischievous, pouting, vivacious. . . ."

I'm not sure that piece could have been much more complimentary had Marie actually written it herself, although from an objective perspective, her positive qualities were really starting to shine. I think we can probably take Marie's looks as read for now, but the twenty-six-year-old readily displayed the refreshing traits of self-deprecation and humility. She was unpretentious, yet ambitious, and grounded—as demonstrated by the simple pastimes she enjoyed away from the rigors of the studio.

The following image comes from the same *Picture-Play* article—the scan may not do complete justice to the magazine original, but it is stunning nevertheless.

Certainly—or at least so far—Marie's reputation had only been temporarily tarnished by marital issues; I could find no trace of "major" scandals, affairs etc., and onscreen, Marie's popularity

continued to grow. She was rumored to be receiving more fan mail than any of Warner's brightest lights of the time, and strong performances were rewarded with glowing reviews, thereby ensuring that the best parts kept coming Marie's way.

However, it seems that Marie's lack of onscreen activity during 1923 may have been instigated, to some extent at least, by Jack Warner—told you he never forgot. Projects scheduled to involve Marie were scrapped and, in addition, Harlan was offered only mediocre parts by his retaining studio.

"Marie was devastated," her sister Peggy was later quoted as saying. Denied any input into scripts, costar, or studio, Marie's rise to prominence was in stark contrast to the way she must have now felt about the job she loved so much.

That said, *Red Lights*—a mystery with a railroad theme—was such a success that two more secretaries had to be employed to cope with the increased volume of mail from fans.

The Wanters was another hit, and by now, Warner was so irritated that he recalled Marie and insisted that esteemed German-born director Ernst Lubitsch find her a role that would deflect away the public attention.

Lubitsch had arrived in Hollywood in 1922, and his reputation was such that the Warner studio tied him to a pretty remarkable deal that gave him full control of cast, crew, and final cut editing of six movies. If he actually made any attempt to appease Warner, Ernst Lubitsch failed heroically as *The Marriage Circle* (again written by Paul Bern) provided Marie with arguably the finest film of her career to date.

The story went that Warner returned from a trip abroad to find that Lubitsch had handed Marie the perfect chance to showcase her talent.

The studio owner threatened to dismiss the director, the writer—and seemingly anyone else who happened to be involved with filming. Jack Warner insisted on numerous re-takes—which Lubitsch invariably discarded—and, according to Lubitsch himself, Warner seemed intent on not only spoiling the film, but far worse, to ruin the career of one of the industry's brightest young stars.

A VERY TAXING TIME

I have seen an extended clip of *The Marriage Circle*—and hopefully I'll get to see the entire film at some point. Marie plays Mizzi Stock, an Austrian (clever ploy in a silent film) who was improbably and unhappily married to the much older Professor Josef Stock (Adolphe Menjou, whose name sounds as though it could be Austrian—but he was American).

Mizzi has her eyes set on Dr. Franz Braun (Monte Blue), husband of her friend Charlotte Braun (Florence Vidor), and by now, you can probably guess where the plot is going.

Flirting, obsession, possible marital breakdown, and new relationships—it's a recipe for disaster—and as you would expect, the movie does not have a happy ending for all the protagonists. Franz and Charlotte's marriage does remain intact, but [*spoiler alert*] Mizzi gets her marching orders just as a reconciliation with Josef looks to be on the cards.

The *Photoplay* review of the film praised Lubitsch for being able to tell a story using pictures and his own vision without having to resort to a title card every few minutes. The simplicity and humanity of the piece were both recognized and praised. The review continued thus:

> *Mr. Lubitsch has been notably economical even in his use of incident. The scenes are laid in Vienna, but there is no attempt at scenic effects. It is just everyday life and surroundings. The cast is uniformly good. It would be hard to award first place to any one of* [the cast]. *The women will probably give it to Miss Prevost, but there is something positively enchanting in the work of Mr. Menjou. He's such a "wise egg."*

I judge films on a more basic level—due almost exclusively to a fundamental lack of culture—but I am able to appreciate that it must have taken tremendous skill to create characters (without audible dialogue) that were rounded, believable and, perhaps most importantly, inspired some emotional connection—be it in a positive or negative way—with the viewer.

The next picture is a scan from *Classic Pictorial of Screen and Stage* magazine (*Motion Picture Classic*) from February 1924. It is a fantastic photograph, which features (from left to right): Adolphe Menjou, Marie Prevost, Ernst Lubitsch, Monte Blue, Florence Vidor, and Creighton Hale.

According to Charles Foster, relationships between the cast became strained when Lubitsch declared: "It is unforgivable that she [Marie] is not the number one star of my film. . . . She steals every scene." At an opening night party, Warner told Lubitsch that he was the only person who could determine star status; Menjou was of the opinion that it was *his* name that drew audiences to theaters, and Florence Vidor was angry enough to throw a drink over the director before storming out. As for Monte Blue, he thought Marie was "sensational."

The photo preceded a feature on Lubitsch, written by Harry Carr, a hugely respected journalist and sports reporter, who had initially risen to prominence with his accounts of the San Francisco earthquake in 1906.

What I found particularly interesting—amusing even—was the way that Lubitsch's words were initially Americanized, but were then amended to Carr's idea of a phonetic transcription of Lubitsch's German accent. I'm not sure I've explained that very well, but an example of the latter will follow shortly.

Lubitsch had admitted that things were difficult when he first arrived in America, shortly after the conclusion of the First World War. He didn't know anyone and his first impression of Hollywood was defined by the weather: drizzling, cold, foggy, and dark. However, Lubitsch readily conceded that he was treated "with kindness and sympathetic cordiality," even though he felt frustrated at having to adapt his first film to please the American audience. But as the German director stated: "This one [*The Marriage Circle*] I am going to make to please Lubitsch."

In doing so, Lubitsch "airily ignored the actresses whom Hollywood had stamped 'great' and picked out a graduate bathing young lady for his great acting part." And this is how the article continued—complete with phonetic German:

> *My peechaar—I don't know if he is good. He can't know about a peechaar until you see him on screen but Marie Prevost she is goot. She is a goot actress—she haf life and animation and she got emotion. But she got hoomer too. No actress is goot in a heavy rôle unless they got a sense of hoomer, especially what you call vamps.*

"Good" even becomes "goot" as Carr does a great—albeit surreal—job of bringing Lubitsch's words to life. As for Marie—whose legs Carr claimed were "the most beautiful in the world"—she was clearly thrilled to be working for Lubitsch: "To act even one scene under his direction is not only an education, but a revelation." She also had the brief opportunity to remember her days as a Bathing Beauty:

> *Over at the Sennett lot, I was one of the few girls who could really swim. I had to double for the girl stars and sometimes I even doubled for the men. In those days, it didn't matter what happened to me if the pulchritude of the real actresses was not damaged. To say the least, life was not monotonous. I never knew whether I was going to be alive or dead at the end of the day.*

As much as Marie might have been a fan of Ernst Lubitsch, she was far less enamored with—wait for it—monkeys, of all things! "Darwin must have been clean crazy when he said we're descended from the hateful little beasts!" Marie told *Photoplay*, in one of the most random articles I've ever seen. Her aversion seems to stem from a childhood trip with her mother to the zoo or circus. Marie was horrified by everything from their "leering faces" to their "claws" and "gestures." The difference between human beings and monkeys couldn't be wider for Marie—"wonderful" to "detestable." "I wish," she declared, "that I might never have to look at another monkey as long as I live."

Probably best to return to the big screen now. Marie (who had shaken off the effects of flu) and Monte Blue were paired together in *How to Educate a Wife*—an apparently forgettable Warner Brothers offering. And the couple featured again in *Daughters of Pleasure*, for which Marie was loaned—or dispatched if your name was Jack Warner—to the lesser studio of Principal Pictures. Amongst the cast was Clara Bow, who would soon be recognized as one Hollywood's best-known and most beautiful actresses.

The Prevost-Blue collaborations continued with *Being Respectable*, and then came *Cornered*—minus Monte. Of the former, the *Pittsburgh Press* of June 29, 1924, admitted that Marie was very much a screen star, but had not perhaps fully appreciated the move from comedy to serious acting. A tendency to clown around had been noted, at times when a particular role, or scene, required a much more serious approach. "That habit," claimed the reviewer, "is a throwback from her early Mack Sennett days, and is being rapidly beaten down as she is made to realize that her possibilities in the line of serious roles are absolutely unlimited."

In contrast—well I think it's in contrast—*Photoplay* considered that Marie's performance had shown "further histrionic improvement."

Marie's next part was that of the wonderfully named Nettie Dark, in *Tarnish*, alongside the dashing Ronald Colman and May McAvoy. Colman played Emmet Carr, who was engaged to Letitia Tevis (McAvoy), but dallying—shall we say—with Nettie, who was threatening to expose their affair and ruin Emmet's relationship with his intended.

The only problem was that Nettie was also involved with Letitia's father Adolph, and humiliation duly followed for the destructive "bad girl."

This film was produced by *Goldwyn Pictures* and Sam Goldwyn apparently duped Jack Warner—someone for whom he cared little—into believing this was another sub-standard script. Warner duly signed a contract believing Marie's career could be further undermined and Goldwyn then unveiled the "real" screenplay, written by the renowned Frances Marion—another success was assured, and Warner was left enraged.

Ernst Lubitsch told Jack Warner that he had a couple of projects set aside for Marie: the films were entitled *Three Women* and *Kiss Me Again*. Lubitsch was making the studio a lot of money, but Jack Warner would not be swayed, and he turned down the director's plans. At this point, Lubitsch reminded Warner that his contract gave him full rights to pick and choose performers as he wished—*Three Women* would be acclaimed as one of Lubitsch's finest pieces of work.

Marie Prevost had become one of silent cinema's biggest attractions, but even though external studios paid Jack Warner a weekly fee in the region of $5,000 for Marie's services, her contract was for $1,500, and that's all Warner was prepared to pay.

Away from the movie set, Marie and Kenneth Harlan were preparing to marry. *Photoplay* commented that, at last, two Hollywood celebrities had been found who were prepared to admit they were engaged. The date had been set for "sometime in the fall" and their October 14 marriage was reported in the *New York Times* on the following day, with some nice additional information in the January 1925 issue of *Photoplay*: The ceremony, which was conducted Dr. John A. Eby, took place at the Wilshire Presbyterian Church. The couple honeymooned in Del Monte, a planned trip to Honolulu having to be canceled owing to Harlan being cast for the leading role in Harold Bell Wright's *The Re-Creation of Brian Kent*.

Guests at the wedding included Mr. and Mrs. Charles Canfield, who were best man and matron of honor respectively, and Harlan's mother Rita attended the ceremony, as did Marie's mother and sister.

Several years later, Marie revealed that Kenneth Harlan had been "wonderful" and "understanding" when he learned that he would have to wait to marry Marie (for reasons previously outlined). This is how she remembered her wedding day:

> *My divorce was granted on a holiday; the next day was a Saturday; we were working and couldn't get to the license bureau before noon; then there was Sunday. They were the three longest days of my existence. Monday we were married. I always had to be married in a church and have a minister and all the trimmings which my child imagination had created for a ceremony so solemn.*

Seemingly, when the bride and groom arrived at the church, they discovered that a camera had been placed on the altar by reporter and future noted gossip columnist Harrison Carroll—who would be later credited for helping Marion Morrison find an altogether more suitable stage name.

Marie approached Carroll and asked if he was married. Carroll answered in the affirmative. Was he happily married? "I guess so," was the reply. Marie reportedly then said: "I work all day long, sometimes all night long in pictures. Won't you please let me get just married without doing it before a camera?"

Carroll duly acceded to Marie's request, prompting the actress to call him "the sweetest man I ever knew."

Anyway, I've decided to save my one magazine scan of the couple for later in the chapter, and their marriage is therefore commemorated on the next page, with a cigarette card from the *Cinema Stars* series—set six—issued by the British American Tobacco Co. in 1927.

Cards from this set with numbers from 102 to 156 are actually quite rare—which is good news, because card no.108 is from my own collection—and it's (relatively) interesting to note that no company name appears anywhere on the cards.

Before 1924 was over, Marie was reunited with Monte Blue in *The Lover of Camille* and *The Black Swan*. The *Evening Independent* edition dated November 29, 1924, included this small piece about the former, to which I have thoughtfully added a couple of helpful little notes:

After the Camille of [Eleonora] *Duse* [the Italian-born actress, who had actually died earlier that year] *and* [Sarah] *Bernhardt,* [Ethel] *Barrymore and* [Alla] *Nazimova* [who was born in what is now Ukraine]*, Marie Prevost's Camille can not be mediocre—and is not, to be sure. Her characterization has something outstanding, something that not every star can accomplish.*

Marie was given the chance to let her fans know how fortunate she felt to have become successful—this quote comes from *Pictures and the Picturegoer* in December 1924:

> *Because I was lucky enough to score a hit in 'The Marriage Circle' I have been given better and better roles from that movie on. I love variety, my Camille in 'The Lover of Camille' is very different from my character in 'Three Women'. And the selfish and rather fast young wife I play in 'The Dark Swan' is very different again. So I thank my lucky stars, and that success, that has not tied me down to one characterization.*

One month earlier, the same magazine had waxed lyrical about Marie—whilst recognizing the huge impact that Ernst Lubitsch had made to her career. E. R. Thomson was clearly a fan of Marie, claiming that it was her quality of what he called "aliveness" that truly engaged audiences. Thomson compared Marie's ability to show every aspect of her own personality in her performances to other—albeit unnamed—screen stars that were "well-schooled" and "artificial." To Thomson, Marie was "a perverse, troubling little person, full of moods and desires, petulant, flattering, and always brimful of life. One instant she will be coaxing, another will find her defiant. But whatever is her mood of the moment, the screen will reflect it with perfect frankness."

Ernst Lubitsch is credited with giving Marie the opportunity to flourish in front of the camera—even if the partnership came as a surprise to many. Her work for Mack Sennett was acknowledged, but it took a man of Lubitsch's vision—and bravery—to both spot and nurture Marie's talent: "Marie had been regarded as a pretty, useful girl with plenty of spirits and ability; a good all-round player with many advantages as an athlete. But a great actress—!"

Thomson described Marie as having a "lively nature," but evidently meant she was temperamental, as he likened her to Pola Negri, the ridiculously gifted Polish-born actress (singer, writer, dancer etc.) with whom Lubitsch had worked closely in Berlin prior to the pair both ending up in Hollywood.

The article concluded by posing a question: Would Marie, with all her qualities, "find a permanent place among the real artists on the screen? Or will she—like so many others before her—find that her very success is her undoing?"

Thomson chose the former.

He would be proved wrong.

The more pieces that offer subjective praise, the stronger my impression becomes that Marie really was bringing something different to the silent screen. In amongst the array of attractive young Sennett belles, Marie was one of the few girls who could actually put the bathing costume to practical use and, as she progressed into the world of credited parts, Marie's lack of formal acting training and her clearly effervescent personality somehow combined to propel her towards stardom—all she needed was the catalyst of influential support, and that came in the form of Ernst Lubitsch.

Seemingly normal service continued into 1925 for the Prevost-Blue onscreen partnership, with the release of *Recompense*. And a nice little sideline appeared in *Motion Picture News*, describing how work to finish *Recompense* had continued through the night so that Marie could spend three days instead of two with her new husband.

Her (in fact their—Monte Blue was alongside Marie once more) next movie was *Kiss Me Again*, directed by Ernst Lubitsch. It was a successful formula, although the *New York Times* review from August 3, did include minor criticism, despite the film apparently being "directed with such ease and charm that one is kept in a merry mood for its full length." The reviewer questioned whether it was time for Lubitsch to tackle "a more serious dramatic subject, something with tense and gripping situations," but did concede that *Kiss Me Again* was "an admirable production, in which one sees Lubitsch's genius."

I do enjoy the way that some reviews offer a one-word analysis of various performances and this *Motion Picture News* extract offers some classic examples: "Miss Prevost and Monte Blue are delightful in their rôles. Mr. Louis is capital as the lawyer DuBois, for which rôle he curled his hair. Mr. Roche is satisfactory as Maurice."

I can just imagine John Roche seeing the words "delightful" and "capital" and eagerly anticipating the positive adjective that was coming his way—only to be hit by "satisfactory," the word a reviewer presumably used when there was nothing good to say.

In April 1925, *Picture and the Picturegoer* devoted a page—sixteen if you happen to be interested—to considering what they described as the "ticklish business" of onscreen love-making, with particular reference to the "delicate situation" of Marie being filmed getting up close and personal with Monte Blue, whilst Kenneth Harlan was doing something similar with a female costar, despite the fact that the real-life couple had only recently married.

The article tried to separate "real" and "simulated" love, between which audiences often struggled to differentiate. Two examples were cited: the first was Beverley Bayne and Francis X. Bushman, who appeared in over twenty films together and would eventually marry—and divorce—in real life. This was contrasted with Marie and Monte Blue who were both married—but simply not to each other.

There then followed a more detailed look at the various types of relationship that Marie and Monte had brought so successfully to the big screen. I'm going to reproduce the two paragraphs using the pretence of interest and appeal to distract from what is little more than laziness on my part:

> In 'The Marriage Circle', you will remember, Marie was the delicious little flirt fluttering on the fringe of 'vamping' and giving Monte palpitations of the heart that he didn't want at all. From that they proceeded straight to 'The Lover of Camille' where Marie inspires in Monte what the French call "grande passion" which she doesn't reciprocate. Change about again for 'The Dark Swan' and Marie hooks and catches Monte with the bait of prettiness and personality and he suffers the equivalent fate to that of the poor fish.
>
> Then once more this pair of lovers become the 'Peter' and 'Julie' of Robert Keable's novel 'Recompence,' [sic] the sequel to 'Simon Called Peter,' in which you no doubt remember Peter is looking round France for something he wants without quite knowing what and finally finds Julie whose sort of sporting offer of herself leads to a bond of sympathy between them. These four films represent stories of four entirely different kinds of loves demanding a difference in what one might call love technique in each instance.

Now seems the opportune moment to unveil my picture of Marie and Kenneth, which has been scanned from the March 1925 issue of *Photoplay*—which certainly costs considerably more now than the cover price of twenty-five cents all those years ago.

The featured photos came under the heading "Just a Little Nest in the Golden West," but the external shot of the couple's Hollywood home was very much on the "lavish" and "massive" side of "little." Another of the pictures featured the newlyweds in a car, with a couple of canine companions—Sinner and Rover. Marie was most certainly a dog lover and her pets even won prizes at shows—viz. ribbons for her three Cairn terriers at the Philadelphia Sesquicentennial International Dog show in 1926.

Before you look it up, it means 150 years.

Anyway, here are Marie and Kenneth on the steps of their home.

Marie would feature in just two more films in 1925: *Bobbed Hair*—alongside her husband—and *Seven Sinners*, the cast including a "blast from the past" in Heinie Conklin. I have unearthed a *New York Times* review of *Bobbed Hair*, the premise of which is that Marie's character Connemara Moore would decide on a hairstyle—basically either a bob, or not—to show the two men in her life which one she wanted to be with: The suspense was maintained right to the end of the film as Connemara assumed the guise of a convent sister, so that the audience, as well as her suitors, could not tell what she had done to her hair.

With Marie receiving so many glowing reviews, it was hardly surprising that her name was regularly in the Tinseltown gossip columns—often for the most trivial or random of reasons—but fame has a downside too. Just over two weeks after the critical acclaim of her performance in *Bobbed Hair* came this headline—in this instance from the *Southeast Missourian*: "Marie Prevost Is Tax Dodger."

> *Los Angeles. Nov. 19. —Marie Prevost, motion picture actress, has been added to the government's list of film stars delinquent in the payment of income taxes. A tax lien was filed against the actress in federal court for $788 alleged loss due on her 1924 income.*

Given the enormous house (and presumably similar-sized wealth) Marie enjoyed with Kenneth Harlan, such a sum would surely have been readily available, and the omission therefore an oversight—but the press weren't going to miss even the smallest opportunity to report some "scandal."

"I didn't have any early struggles—until now," Marie later said, rather ironically. "They're just beginning."

Seven films from 1926 are listed on the *IMDb* site for Marie, but it is almost certain that she did not feature at all in one of them: *Nana*. This movie was filmed in France, but so regular were press mentions of Marie's comings and goings in America, that it seems unfeasible that she would have had the time travel to Europe for a starring role, let alone the minor part of Gaga. All of which means the 120 movies quoted earlier should now read 119—probably.

1926 began with surgery for Marie—*The Berkeley Daily Gazette* of January 5, reporting that: "Marie Prevost was rapidly recuperating today from the effects of an abdominal operation at the Hollywood hospital. The star will be able to leave the hospital within a week, it was stated by attending physicians."

There were also stories of another change of studio for Marie. Under the headline "The Warner Stampede," *Motion Picture News* remarked that "actors and actresses [*one of whom was Marie*] are quitting the Warner Studio in carload lots." The short article ended humorously—or at least it tried: "It is also rumored that Rin-tin-tin has threatened to quit the company unless it accedes to his demands of an increase of ten bones a week."

This may suggest Marie's departure was voluntary, but over a decade later, Marie's long-time friend Phyllis Haver told a magazine that Warner's rejection was one of the causes of problems in Marie's marriage—Marie sought solace in alcohol, and Harlan (who had also left Warner Brothers) became every bit as addicted to gambling.

The trade press confirmed that Marie had been offered a deal with Metropolitan Studios, and she would star in a number of films that would be released through the comparatively unknown—and ultimately short-lived—Producers Distributing Corporation (whose convention Marie attended later that year). However, her first two releases in 1926 *His Jazz Bride* and *The Caveman* were both Warner productions—and both featured Matt Moore alongside Marie. The latter film was released on February 6, the date when the papers revealed the news that would arguably change Marie's life forever. The headline in the *Berkeley Daily Gazette* revealed the shocking news: "Film Star's Mother Killed, Two Injured."

On February 5, Hughina Prevost was killed in a car accident on the way to Florida to visit Marie. The article that follows appeared in the *Youngstown Vindicator*, and details the terrible injuries sustained by Marie's mother, but only mentions two of the three other people who were in the vehicle at the time of the crash, which occurred near Lordsburg, New Mexico.

> *Los Angeles, Cal., Feb. 6. —Mrs H. Prevost, mother of Marie Prevost, the film star, was killed, and Al Christie, screen comedy producer, and Vera Steadman, motion picture actrett [sic], were injured in an automobile accident last night, near Lordsburg, N.M., according to word received here early today.*
>
> *The car, a heavy machine owned by Miss. Steadman, overturned at 30 miles an hour, the massage said. Mrs. Prevost suffered a broken spine and a fractured skull, dying before medical aid could be summoned.*

> *Christie and the actress narrowly escaped death, being pinned under the machine. Both were rescued by occupants of a passing car.*
>
> *The party was bound for Palm Beach to visit Miss. Prevost.*

Al Christie suffered deep cuts to his head and left arm—Hughina appears to have been sitting in the passenger seat. In the back seats were not only the actress and former Sennett Bathing Beauty Vera Steadman—who was also the car's owner and was intending to enter her motor boat *Baby Mine* in races being held at Palm Beach later in February—but also (and, perhaps bizarrely), A. Todd, described elsewhere as a "chauffeur." The former had a leg injury, but Todd seemingly escaped unscathed from the wreck of the open-topped vehicle.

The *Los Angeles Times* on February 10, revealed that the "wheel on their automobile broke and the car turned over"—it was actually one of the back wheels. The article also confirmed that the (unnamed) chauffeur "escaped uninjured"; there is no suggestion that someone else was actually behind the wheel, but Mr. Todd was apparently due to be Vera Steadman's boat mechanic.

On page sixteen of the same paper was Hughina's formal death notice:

> *PREVOST - At Lordsburg, NM, February 1926, Mrs H Prevost, beloved mother of Mrs Marie Prevost Harlan and Marjorie Prevost. Funeral services will be held at the Little Church of the Flowers, Forest Lawn Cemetery, Thursday, February 11, at 2 o'clock p.m.. G A Fitch, director.*

Marie had not yet reached her thirtieth birthday, but she had lost both her parents in truly awful circumstances. Time would tell that Marie was badly affected by this bereavement, and the implications on the rest of her life would be hugely significant.

Next comes a now poignant picture of Marie and her mother, which appeared in *Motion Picture* magazine during 1925.

It was around this point in her life when Marie supposedly—in a salt kind of way—entered into an affair with producer Howard Hughes, who was almost ten years her junior.

According to Darwin Porter's book *Howard Hughes: Hell's Angel*, the pair became close through talking about the untimely

deaths of their respective mothers. The inference was that during their brief relationship (which Hughes ended), he "liberated" Marie sexually—you can make of that what you will. There was also an allegation that Marie had slept with Adolphe Menjou, with whom she had appeared in *The Marriage Circle*.

Whilst researching this book, I didn't find any other references to that particular liaison, nor to any high-profile affairs involving Marie: suffice to say this was 1920s Hollywood and anything could—and often did—happen.

Despite all the upheaval, Marie was still quite busy, and she appeared in *Other Women's Husbands* with Monte Blue, and *Up in Mabel's Room*, which was Marie's first film for her new distributor. It was produced by the *Christie Film Company*, which had been created by Canadian-born brothers Al and Charles Christie—the former you will remember had been driving the car when Marie's mother was killed.

In the film, Marie played the eponymous Mabel Ainsworth alongside an actor with a very familiar name: Harrison Ford—apparently no relation. Ford portrayed Mabel's husband Garry, and the plot was concerned with the pair's (or rather Mabel's) attempts at reconciliation. I have seen a short, but brilliant, clip of the couple on a night out together. Mabel was flirting outrageously and Garry actually looked scared to death!

When they sat down, she casually moved her chair closer, and Garry immediately shifted his further away. Mabel then started playing footsie under the table prompting Garry to hurriedly lift his feet off the floor. He waved his handkerchief in front of his face as the temperature rose: "Nice and cool isn't it?" smiled Mabel.

"Not where I'm sitting," came the flustered reply.

Marie plays "sexy" very convincingly—it's not all in the eyes, but they remained incredibly expressive. *Photoplay* described her performance simply as "good," adding "The story drags slightly—taken as it is from a play that depends on clever lines for applause."

Almost a Lady, with Harrison Ford, and *For Wives Only*—based on the play *The Critical Year*—brought the curtain down on 1926, but for all the fame and adoration she had received as her career blossomed, I am sure Marie Prevost would have swapped everything simply to have her mother back.

WHAT'S THE FREQUENCY, KENNETH?

You should probably guess you're in for a bad year when some hairdresser called Antoine tells the world your hairstyle is "cute, but a little artificial and unnatural."

A lengthy feature on the "bob" appeared in *Photoplay* at the start of 1927, and on the basis that resident hair expert Antoine claimed that the attractive and eminently fashionable Colleen Moore's "Dutch-boy" cut made her face look vulgar, Marie arguably got off lightly.

On a much more serious level, as 1927 progressed, it became evident that Marie's marriage had completely disintegrated. It was reported that Kenneth Harlan regularly stayed out on all night drinking and gambling sessions—he squandered thousands of dollars and even forged Marie's signature on a check after he'd emptied his own account.

Marie herself was struggling to come to terms with the events of the previous twelve months as well as her marital troubles. What was initially comfort from alcohol had developed into a dependency. *Photoplay* also claimed that Marie had started collecting stamps—arguably irrelevant, but I still thought I'd include it.

She still had her looks, but she was no longer contracted to a major and influential studio—talking films were just around the corner and would have a massive impact on the movie industry and the players in it. Marie was haunted by the demons of two deaths, yet Hollywood—and movie fans—demanded a brave face and scandal-free existence as the price of fame and fortune. The essence of celebrity that forms such a part of modern-day culture may have been in its relative infancy in the late 1920s, but it existed nonetheless and exerted a pressure that whilst intangible, could still have a dramatic effect on those who wanted—in fact needed—to keep their professional head above water.

With virtually no close relatives and a wholly unreliable husband, there must have been times when she didn't know quite where to turn—except towards the bottle. And when the moment of realization dawned that she was loved by thousands yet essentially alone, it must have been incredibly hard to deal with—in fact Marie never really did deal with it.

The *Milwaukee Journal* from October 16, 1927, confirmed that Marie had filed for divorce, citing mental cruelty and alleging that Harlan had a jealous nature and would often tell Marie that he should have married someone else instead. Tellingly, the short paragraph ended by indicating the couple had separated as long ago as May 1926.

As if that wasn't enough, Marie was injured during work on *The Rush Hour*, when she was thrown from an aquaplane at Catalina Island. She needed to take a few days off filming and she also spent time in hospital during 1927. One article in the first half of the year revealed that Marie had been chosen to be the Fresno Mardi Gras Queen for a day—quite an honor apparently—and that she had recovered from a minor operation. Then, in October 1927, there was a further mention of Marie having had surgery—I do not know whether these reports related to the same or different operations.

Just over a month later, another of Milwaukee's newspapers, the *Sentinel*, reported several anticipated changes to Marie's divorce case, including "asserted drinking" by Harlan and a particular party he had organized. Marie explained that complaints about Harlan's regular parties had been made by neighbors, and that being woken at four o'clock in the morning and coming downstairs to be greeted by a number of bathing-suit clad young women was basically the final straw.

Marie also claimed that Harlan was in the habit of ringing during the early hours "saying he was coming home, and then not coming," or calling almost every hour from his all-night drinking parties to let his wife know what a good time he was having!

The paper also quoted May 19, 1926, as being the day the couple separated, and that Judge Fletcher Bowron had indicated that he would grant the divorce. I doubt it was a tough decision.

Aspects of these last two articles make quite disturbing reading. If Marie had left Harlan in May 1926—the exact date notwithstanding— that would be just over three months after her mother had been killed.

The trauma of the loss of her only remaining parent must have been so intense, yet from the available facts, Harlan seemingly displayed an almost callous disregard for his wife's feelings, choosing selfish indulgence instead.

Whilst giving a gentle nod towards the fact that there are two sides to every story, I had a quick glance at Kenneth Harlan's biography. He married a total of *eight* times—and perhaps that's proof enough that despite numerous attempts, Harlan simply wasn't ideal husband material.

Marie continued to work through the heartache—*Man Bait* saw her play shop assistant Madge Dreyer, who was fired after rejecting her boss's advances, and she then duly obtained work as a dancer. There she met Jeff Sanford who (for the plot) was the son of her former boss. The pair fell in love, but his family disapproved of the relationship—actually that's not entirely true, as Jeff's brother Gerald (Kenneth Thomson) was equally smitten and with Jeff moving back into higher social circles, Gerald ended up with Madge.

The *Photoplay* review reckoned that Marie's character "is one of those good little sales-ladies who smashes a masher and is promptly fired." I had to look it up, but I believe that a "masher" was a man who gave a woman unwanted attention—and "smashing" was a proactive way of dealing with it!

Anyway, the subsequent release was entitled *Getting Gertie's Garter* (which was about Gertie . . . and a garter). *The Night Bride* (with Harrison Ford) came next, followed by another appearance alongside Ford in *The Girl on the Train*, which is also known as *The Girl in the Pullman*. Marie's first films of 1928 were *On to Reno*—slightly ironic given her own situation, with the Nevadan city being known as the "divorce capital of the world"—and *A Blonde for a Night* in which Marie's character became (somewhat bizarrely) unrecognizable to her husband Bob (Harrison Ford) simply by donning a blonde wig.

The following scanned image appeared in *Photoplay* to mark the release of *On to Reno*—"Marie Prevost still wears her wedding ring," states the caption, "which means that Marie and Kenneth Harlan aren't at all sure they want to make their separation a legal one."

Movie number three from 1928 gives me the perfect opportunity for a review of a Marie Prevost film I've actually seen. First of all, there is a short clipping from the *Pittsburgh Post Gazette*, dated April 5, 1928, regarding Marie's casting in the film *The Racket*.

Three things before you read it: "Tommy" is actor Thomas Meighan, "Irene" is actually called Helen in the film and, from what I've read, *The Godless Girl* was released in two versions—the silent movie in August 1928 and a part-sound version in March 1929. For the purposes of this book, I am sticking with the film order offered by *IMDb*, although I fully accept the vagaries and possible inaccuracies of that particular source. In addition, *The Racket* originally premièred on June 30, 1928—but wasn't actually released until November that year—so somehow I think I've almost justified why I'm dealing with *The Racket* before *The Godless Girl*—almost:

> *Both he and Howard Hughes have searched and searched for the right girl to play opposite Tommy in 'The Racket' and it now seems their long search has been rewarded. Marie Prevost has been signed by Caddo Company to play the part of Irene, an underworld character and the only woman in the picture.*
>
> *Tommy is enthusiastic over the idea too. He feels she is just the type. Marie has only lately finished in the Cecil DeMille picture, 'The Godless Girl' and someone who stole a peep at the picture tells me Marie comes pretty near stealing the show. She has gotten much thinner and that blond wig has worked wonders for her, on screen at least.*

Marital and weight-related matters will have to wait for a while—because next is my look back at *The Racket*.

KICKING UP A RACKET

The Racket is a film adaptation of Bartlett Cormack's work of the same name—directed by Lewis Milestone and produced by Marie's alleged erstwhile lover Howard Hughes. The movie has the distinction of being nominated for what was then called Best Picture, Production, at the first ever Academy Awards ceremony, which was held in May the following year—the Oscar was actually won by a movie entitled *Wings*—and it is also the first full-length silent film that I have ever watched.

Thomas Meighan stars as Captain McQuigg, intent on bringing the powerful bootlegger Nick Scarsi (Louis Wolheim) to justice. Wolheim has "gangster" written all over him. With a nose flattened courtesy of a sporting injury, his look was intimidating (he was by no means a handsome man), but the former teacher turned actor was a fine and well-respected performer. As far as Marie Prevost was concerned, she took the part of Helen Hayes, a singer—and a feisty one at that.

The film opens with McQuigg and Scarsi meeting in a dark doorway—it soon becomes clear that the "racket" in which Scarsi is involved is alcohol related and he's about to tread on the toes of fellow bootlegger Spike Corcoran (Henry Sedley). Scarsi warns McQuigg to let the rival gangs sort out the situation between them and duly invites the police officer to a party being held for his younger brother Joe that evening.

Over on Eighth and Grand, Scarsi's operation doesn't quite go according to plan: several people get shot and one of Scarsi's associates, Chick (Lucien Prival) is arrested. News of the events is phoned through to the newspaper editor, at which point one single word appears on screen: "Pratt!"

Well I think that's a bit harsh—he was only ringing to tell you about "the big killing on Eighth and Grand. . . ."

Of course, Pratt is actually a reporter (played by Lee Moran) and his drunken sidekick Miller was portrayed by Richard "Skeets" Gallagher. The duo manages to provide some light comic relief throughout the film.

Over at the Scarsis' bash, Joe (George Stone) couldn't look more different to his brother: Nick is tall, thick-set and ugly, whereas Joe is small, scrawny and . . . ugly; so there is at least one similarity.

Well aware that Chick is in custody, Nick Scarsi rings McQuigg to remind him about the party.

"I'll be there," replies McQuigg—well he would have done if the film hadn't been silent—the same words he'd used about the earlier drop.

Two masked dancers are performing at this point; they leave the floor and the girl removes her mask to reveal . . . Helen Hayes, played by a blonde and beautiful Marie Prevost.

Helen is draped across a piano, which is wheeled across to the Scarsi table. She begins to sing to Joe and move provocatively towards him. Nick Scarsi angrily kicks away the piano—and Helen is not happy. Bravely—or foolishly depending on your point of view—she confronts Scarsi: "You can get away with murder, but you can't pull that stuff on me."

Scarsi gets to his feet, manhandles the blonde chanteuse and humiliates her in front of the guests, calling her a "gold-digger."

McQuigg arrives and is ushered over to Scarsi's table; he has been placed next to Chick and smugly tears up Chick's place-name, only for Scarsi's sidekick, newly released from jail, to tap the police officer even more smugly on the shoulder.

Spike Corcoran and some of his henchmen gatecrash the party. Scarsi has a gun under the table, which is trained on his rival—the mood is actually very tense, in stark contrast to the jovial music being played by the band. Scarsi fires and kills Corcoran, but even though the police have turned up in numbers, Scarsi's men manage to hide the murder weapon.

Despite the fundamental lack of evidence, McQuigg arrests Scarsi, but a writ of *habeas corpus* gains Scarsi his freedom. For the record, *habeas corpus* is a Latin phrase literally meaning "may you have the body." Essentially it is a legal release from illegal detention—well it's supposed to be!

The extent of the influence that Scarsi is able to exert is demonstrated when McQuigg is suddenly transferred to the wilds of Twenty-Eighth Precinct. Reporters Pratt and Miller soon arrive, eager to get McQuigg's story—as is Ames (John Darrow), a young journalist, who is equally keen to make an impression. The more experienced pairing attend Spike's funeral and whisper—loudly enough for Scarsi to overhear—that Scarsi had instigated the transfer because he was scared of McQuigg, and it got the intended reaction from the flat-nosed villain.

Presumably not too much later, Joe and Helen are on a driving date. Joe has one thing on his mind—and Helen isn't planning on saying "yes" anytime soon. Joe pushes an engagement ring onto Helen's finger—albeit on her right hand—and assumes that Marie will now swoon at his feet.

He is mistaken, and when his advances are rebuffed, Joe does the honorable thing and orders Helen out of the car. Luckily a passing police officer is on hand and goes to have a quiet word with Joe.

Scarsi junior panics, drives off at high speed, and knocks down a woman before crashing the car.

Not surprisingly, Joe is invited down to the station (by Patrolman Johnson, played by Pat Collins)—McQuigg's new station at is happens. Helen arrives and is soon dispatched to the cells herself, Marie's use of facial expressions during these scenes is fantastic—as is the moment when she is escorted away by the arresting officer, and simply links arms with him!

By now, the viewer is in no doubt that novice reporter Ames is totally besotted with Helen, and despite her brash exterior, she does seem to have something of a soft(ish) centre.

I didn't quite get the next bit: Joe won't reveal his name—eventually he offers "Joe Camino," presumably to avoid any connection with his brother. Yet Captain McQuigg was not only at Joe's party but he also sat on the same table, so I'm surprised he didn't recognize Joe when he was brought to the station.

No matter; Joe is quickly bailed and he, along with District Attorney Welch—Sam DeGrasse's character is another in Scarsi's employ—comes down to Helen's cell to gloat. Joe makes it clear that Helen is going to stay behind bars while he walks free, and the singer responds by taking off the "engagement" ring and giving it to one of her fellow cellmates.

Enraged, Joe tells Helen that his brother will "take care" of her if she doesn't keep her mouth shut, but this next picture shows that the hardened woman was far from terrified by the threat.

There is a nice scene as Ames arrives with various bits and pieces for Helen: a comb, toothbrush, toothpaste, talcum powder, as well as a dowdy nightdress—and, once again, Marie's wonderful eyes say it all.

With Helen now prepared to testify against Joe, Nick Scarsi appears and speaks with Johnson. He asks who the officer was who picked up Joe: "I am," replies Johnson—bad move. The officer doesn't know Scarsi and doesn't have many nice things to say about the man who just happens to be about six inches from his face.

Johnson turns his back and Scarsi shoots him. The gangster flees, punching Ames to the floor as he exits stage right.

With Helen released, she joins McQuigg, Welch, and other officers with the injured Ames and stricken Johnson. The director cuts to a wide shot as Johnson's death is confirmed—and the emotion or the power of the moment is enhanced by this piece of camera work.

When questioned, Nick Scarsi claims that he'd sent in his driver to see Helen Hayes. McQuigg replies that he thought Scarsi's driver was in jail—but in a moment of heavy irony it is suggested that any Scarsi associate ends up in a penitentiary "with revolving doors!"

There was only one witness to Johnson's murder—Ames—but he does not know Nick Scarsi. That said, he could—and duly does—identify Scarsi as the man who shot Johnson, and the gangster is arrested. As expected, before you can say *habeas corpus*, a writ arrives, but McQuigg simply rips up the paperwork and locks up Scarsi anyway.

An upcoming election leaves Welch with a dilemma: release Scarsi and bad publicity will surely follow, keep him incarcerated and Ames will pay a heavy price for agreeing to testify—the District Attorney might also pay a heavier price than a simple election defeat.

Helen is also worried for Ames's safety, and, in another cute-to-flat nose-to-nose confrontation, she manages to elicit a confession from Scarsi.

Welch refuses Scarsi the release he's expecting, but a "fixed" window offers Scarsi a potential escape route. However, in another dramatic wide-angle stand-off, Scarsi's impending leap for liberty ends with a fatal bullet.

Miller and Pratt burst in, and Pratt's question about why Scarsi was shot allows an amusing bit of drunken philosophy from Miller: "So that government of the professionals, by the professionals, and for the professionals, shall not perish from the earth."

I couldn't agree more.

Helen lets down Ames gently, and the pair part with a friendly handshake before she and an exhausted McQuigg talk for a minute—they've got more in common than they would have imagined, and, well, that's all folks!

I have to admit that I *really* enjoyed this movie. I wasn't sure what to expect as a silent film virgin, but I actually found the plot easy to follow; characters and storylines perhaps need a little more substance given the lack of dialogue, but the pivotal figures in the movie were definitely well realized. I apologize in advance if, at any point, I try to sound even vaguely like a film critic—my knowledge is far too limited, but hopefully a subjective opinion is of some passing interest.

What struck me most was the range of expressions that some of the actors were capable of. Marie herself was as good as anyone—it wasn't just her eyes (ahh those eyes) or her facial expressions in general, it was also her body language. I hadn't appreciated how much could be conveyed by just small physical movement.

Louis Wolheim was superb too. His appearance and presence were naturally imposing; you can scowl all you want, but sometimes there's nothing more menacing than a smile.

With talking pictures in their infancy—*The Jazz Singer* had been released the previous year—fundamental changes must have been necessary for many of the performers. The advent of sound will have ruined the careers of some, and others will surely have needed to adapt their style in front of the cameras. To a greater or lesser extent, dialogue must have replaced some of those nuances that were crucial in silent films. I will repeat that I am absolutely not an expert, but, for me, the audience will have appreciated the skills of the actor far more *because* they weren't distracted by any words. Is it harder to deliver a purely physical performance? I don't know, but after watching *The Racket*, I have no doubt that one ex-Bathing Beauty had developed into a fine actress.

The film highlighted the era of prohibition, a period during which gang leaders wielded enormous power and influence. Corruption, even amongst those in authority, was not uncommon, and although Captain McQuigg's integrity was beyond question, witness just how easy it was for Scarsi to arrange his transfer simply by being able to manipulate someone in higher office—viz. District Attorney Welch.

The extent of that control, or perceived control, was shown towards the end of the film when, despite having been arrested for a murder he had not only committed, but was seen committing, Scarsi was nothing less than supremely confident that he would walk, basically because he had Welch in his proverbial pocket and the all-important election was looming.

I was going to say that in this film, Marie Prevost reminded me of Jean Harlow; the physical resemblance clearly owed much to the hair color, but although the respective characters were from opposite sides of the legal tracks, I felt there were some similarities between Helen Hayes and Gwen Allen (Jean's part in *The Public Enemy* (1931)).

Perhaps it is because both stories involved boot-legging, featured a beautiful blonde, and were released in the "pre-Code" era when movies contained far more violence and criminal activity than would be permitted under the 1934 Hays Code.

Or is it even more basic than that? Did a movie where law-breaking and scenes of brutality benefit from the attractive moll, dame, call her what you will, to provide something contrastingly pleasing on the eye? Let's be honest, Mack Sennett had already proved as much over a decade earlier.

And here endeth my synopsis and review of *The Racket*. Whether or not it is representative of the genre, I found the film to be a thoroughly watchable piece of late 1920s cinema. Given the fairly recent trauma in her personal life—and in view of what was to follow—this movie proves (to me at least) that Marie Prevost was not only beautiful but also a genuinely gifted performer.

DEPRESSION SETS IN

Before the chapter gets properly underway, here are three cards from a set issued in France during the 1920s. The cards were issued anonymously—almost certainly with packets of biscuits—in France, probably during the late 1920s.

Anyway, back to Marie's marriage, and various cuttings from late 1927 and into the following year indicated that their separation was not quite as final as had been initially reported. "And news trickles round that Marie and Kenneth Harlan are going to call it quits and make up," commented *Pictureplay*, and another article claimed that the couple had been "pleading with the judge not to make the interlocutory decree final." Towards the end of August, Marie and Kenneth left Chicago together, for an engagement in Salt Lake City—and this reinforced the state of their relationship, which was mentioned in *Photoplay*, following the passing of silent actor Ward Crane, who died of pneumonia, aged thirty-eight, in July 1928. According to the magazine: "Undoubtedly the reconciliation of Marie Prevost and Kenneth Harlan was a blow to him for he had been in love with Marie for Many years."

Marie mentioned her friendship with Crane in a revealing *Motion Picture* magazine feature, in which the actress talked at length about her life and loves, but for now, despite all appearances to the contrary, this is how the *Milwaukee Journal* from January 13, 1929, reported Marie's divorce:

> *Los Angeles, Calif.—Marie Prevost, film star and former bathing beauty, was granted a final decree of divorce from Kenneth Harlan, screen actor, in superior court, Saturday. Miss Prevost accused her former husband 'of throwing wild parties' and making fun of her career as a bathing beauty.*
>
> *Chicago—Kenneth Harlan, here on business, said Saturday that he and Marie Prevost were 'the best of friends, but simply could not get on together.'*

However Marie felt about the split, she seemed to handle the situation reasonably well in public—"with a grain of salt and a witty outlook," as reported in the trade press. Marie had not only saved both her wedding rings but they had also been soldered together to make what was described as "an attractive and unusual ornament."

Nipping back to 1928, Marie featured in two more movies: *The Sideshow* (with "Little" Billy Rhodes) and *The Rush Hour*, but the year ended with the actress succumbing to a flu epidemic that had swept across California. I have seen two newspaper reports, both from November 30, one—in the *Evening Independent*—claimed Marie was "considerably improved," whereas the *Milwaukee Sentinel* stated: "A new name was added to the list of film stars who are absent from their work because of illness when Marie Prevost succumbed to an attack of pneumonia and was removed from her home to a hospital. Miss Prevost, according to physicians, is the only one of the absent luminaries who is seriously ill."

I've now reached one of those moments where I have a choice about what to cover next: more of Marie's thoughts on love, or her appearance in *The Godless Girl*. Most writers would go for some carefully considered approach, but my method is slightly less professional—it involves a coin. Heads for affairs of the heart, tails for the movie. . . .

Love it is then.

Marie believed—or at least she did in Ruth Biery's feature that appeared in *Motion Picture* magazine towards the end of the decade—that love was the most misused word in the English language. True love might happen only two or three times in a lifetime, but Marie felt that the term was coined whenever a man and a woman went out together in Hollywood.

Having already mentioned Marie's brief marriage to Sonny Gerke earlier in the book, it is clear that the feelings for her second husband, Kenneth Harlan, lasted longer—well, a little bit longer: "It took seven months, finally after two years together, for the love to fade. In my mind I knew it was going, but I kept clinging to my illusions. My heart, my soul wouldn't admit that my second dream had been blasted."

As indicated before, there was a reconciliation of sorts after the initial separations but, in Marie's words: "you cannot build new fires on old ashes."

During her time apart from Harlan, Marie admitted to spending a lot of time with Ward Crane, a man she described as "wonderful" and "an older person who understood me and my problems."

The age gap was actually only six years, so whilst Crane was undeniably "older," the difference may have been exaggerated by him being "wiser?" Marie talked of Crane as being one of the best friends she had ever had, and she hoped that he felt likewise—irrespective of how the magazines viewed Crane's feelings towards her. Marie claimed she'd known Crane was dying—and suggested that in his time of need, his so-called friends deserted him. In fact, Marie said she was the only person who realized the seriousness of Crane's illness and hoped that her comfort and friendship has enabled her friend to "forget the unkindness of others."

If Marie was as good a friend to Ward Crane as she says, well firstly that serves to reinforce what I believe to be her genuine caring nature, but is there also a chance that such devotion to a friend, that others had seemingly cast aside, simply strengthened whatever feelings Crane may have had for the actress to something—in his eyes—beyond friendship?

It is clear that as well as craving companionship in the aftermath of her separation, Marie also wanted enjoyment in her life—to "go places and see things." But, in what may be a slight generalization, she considered that "all men are the same."

She explained: "The boys who take me out one night and say, 'Oh, you're the most wonderful creature I've ever seen,' take Phyllis Haver out the next night and say the same things to her." Such men were therefore considered "playmates," and love was not on the menu. Interestingly, Marie then added: "Contrary to the verdict of the world, I have found plenty of men in Hollywood who are content to be just pals and darn good friends to a woman."

Hang on—aren't all men the same?!

The feature closed with Marie in a pensive mood: "Perhaps my love is not complete. I hope not. I'd hate to think that I could never fall in love again."

There'll be more chance to dissect Marie's thoughts later on, but it's now time to concentrate on the professional aspect of her life, and it's probably fair to say that the (re-)release of *The Godless Girl* early in 1929 must have been a significant moment for Marie. It was a massive and lavish production—directed by the famed Cecil B. DeMille—that was many months in the making, and Marie must have been hoping that commercial success might bring some respite from her recent illness and the ongoing battle with her personal demons.

Before I look at the movie itself, it is worth spending a bit of time looking through the cast list. The characters are not named—simply described and preceded by the definite article: The Girl, The Other Girl, The Boy, The Brute, The Goat, The Victim et al.

I can tell you that "The Girl" (played by Lina Basquette) was named Judith Craig, and by the time *The Godless Girl* was released, Lina was already a widow—her husband Sam Warner (cofounder of the Warner Brothers studio) had died in 1927. Warner was twenty years Lina's senior, and during their brief marriage, the couple had a daughter whom they named Lita.

Lina's personal life would make a book all of its own—multiple marriages (including one to a cameraman she met on the set of this film!), suicide attempts, an affair with the heavyweight boxing champion Jack Dempsey etc.—but for now, this young doe-eyed beauty was simply Judy, who absolutely didn't believe in God.

"The Boy" was the devoutly religious Bob Hathaway, portrayed by Tom Keene—under his birth name of George Duryea—and "The Goat" was the nickname of Samuel "Bozo" Johnson, played by Eddie Quinlan, who provided most of the movie's lighter-hearted moments.

At its most basic level, the story revolves around the relationship between Judy and Bob, whose beliefs are from opposite ends of the religious spectrum.

The film is full of blatant morality, and the action or plot centers around two genuinely impressive scenes; the first occurs early on in the film and is a mass brawl between members of Judy's Atheist Society and Bob's group of "believers." The fighting breaks out from the meeting hall onto a staircase that extends over several floors; the action is dramatic and has the stark realism possible in pre-code cinema.

The conflict ends when a girl falls through the staircase to her death, although there is still time for the poignant, but not unexpected, moment when the girl questions her lack of faith and wants there to be "something more" than just "the end."

Judy and Bob are duly arrested as the instigators of the violence that led to the accident and taken to the reformatory.

Enter Marie as inmate and "Other Girl," Mame, whose first scene involves chopping clumps of Judy's hair. There are a few comic asides—most, as I said, provided by "Bozo"—but these only serve to provide a greater contrast with the harshness of the regimented penal system.

The main protagonists quickly fall foul of authority, with Bob being subjected to a prolonged soaking from a large hose, the dousing being gleefully delivered by the head guard, "The Brute," played by Noah Beery—brother of 1932 Best Actor Oscar winner Wallace Beery.

Actor Tom Keene could not be doubled for this scene, which was exhausting to film for the actor; it was worse for Eddie Quillan though, who was pushed into a pool of water in which there were exposed electric cables. The shock apparently lifted Quillan into the air.

Anyway, the reward for Bob and Judy's defiance of the regime is a transfer to garbage detail—the irony isn't lost: "What a laugh! Your belief and my blasphemy, both ending in garbage!"

Mame is seen flirting with Bob, and at this point it is clear—actually it was obvious right from the start—that Judy has strong feelings towards her religious rival. It was also evident that Marie had become fuller of face—the noticeable external effect of her alcohol consumption.

A scene follows where Bob and Judy's feelings begin to surface; they place their hands on the wire fence that separates them, and "The Brute," who is watching on, switches on the power to electrify the fence. It is a callous act and actually quite brutally shocking—pardon the unintended pun—to watch, given the fact that the movie is over eighty years old.

The result is solitary confinement for Bob and a cross-shaped scar of none-too-subtle religious significance for Judy.

Judy and Mame retire to bed—both have one of Bob's work gloves, symbols of their growing love for the same man.

There is another vicious episode in which "Bozo" is beaten by "The Brute," before Bob manages to escape from solitary confinement and "acquire" a horse and cart bound for the meat house, where Judy and Mame are now working. Bob tells Mame of his plan to break out of the reformatory; she is thrilled—until she realizes he intends to free Judy as well. For his part, Bob seems totally oblivious to Mame's feelings.

Mame drops several trays of eggs to cause a diversion, and Bob and Judy make good their escape. Freedom affords time both for reflection and to fall in love, but a first kiss is rudely interrupted by a woof from one of the hounds that are now well and truly on their tail. Recapture is only a matter of time, and not only are the pair thrown into solitary confinement—actually that should read *separate* solitary confinement—they are handcuffed (in Judy's case to a pipe) to guarantee detention.

The direction of the film, however, changes completely on the wholly innocent intervention of a black cat. Unceremoniously sent packing by "The Brute," the cat knocks over a lamp, which starts a fire in what appears to be a laundry basket on the girls' side of the prison.

The female inmates see a chance for their own collective freedom, and they turn off the water to ensure there is no swift conclusion to the unfolding drama. Mame realizes Judy is confined in solitary, but the keys are wrestled from her by frenzied inmates who trap her between a metal fence and gate.

Characters and characteristics now unfold rapidly—a released Bob hurries to Judy's aide, but "The Brute," who has the keys that would liberate her, tries to run and save himself. A fight ensues, and his cowardice is "rewarded" with a reciprocal electrocution. The bully begs for his life, Bob snatches the keys and sets Judy free, just as retribution is completed by a collapse of masonry, which traps the now pathetic guard. Mame and "Bozo" appear, and the anticipated moment of indecision results in "The Brute" being rescued and everyone escaping from the inferno.

The dying guard takes his final chance at redemption by recommending to the inspector that those who had attempted to save him should be released.

And this hugely moral, but equally clichéd, tale ends with the "heading off into the sunset" moment for Judy and Bob, whose differences have been overcome by the power of love—ahhh! Mame declines the offer to join the couple: "Three ain't a couple—it's a calamity!"

And that's just about that. Decent film—actually a very good film—with an albeit predictable ending, following a truly spectacular fire sequence, which was staged on a massive studio set constructed by Mitchell Leisen. To make the scenes realistic, the actual set was burned down—three female extras were quite badly injured and Lina Basquette's eyebrows were singed so badly that they never grew back.

If that little piece of trivia is interesting, this next bit is a gem: in amongst the fan letters that Lina Basquette received was one telling how she was the writer's favorite actress.

The sender was Adolf Hitler.

Reviews were generally positive. *Photoplay* believed the film contained "some of the finest scenes any director has done"—namely the death fall, the escape, and the dramatic fire—the trio being described as "exquisite gems." Edwin Schallert of *Motion Picture News* noted: "DeMille has several moments that are amongst his most brilliant theatrically. It [*the film*] is full of tense and exciting incident all closely woven into the story."

The *Milwaukee Sentinel* also published a nice piece shortly after the release of the fully silent version of *The Godless Girl* (the edition was dated September 2, 1928). In the article, Marie discussed her departure from what the paper described as "bedroom farces."

> *You know how an actress can play one kind of role so long that she is never thought of in connection with anything else. It seems I have done nothing but play bedroom farces. And after*

you've played two or three of them, they're all alike. You hide and you get chased and you fall down. I've hidden in so many places that I don't think there's anything left to hide in.

Regarding the filming of the movie, Marie commented: "Even then my past rose up to hit me. Someone thought I ought to do one of my comedy falls. But Mr. DeMille was merciful and that suggestion was out." The article continued to say that Marie is "on tender-hooks until her following sends word as to what it thinks of her work...."

Well, whilst the religious subject matter of the film and the violence—especially generated by faith—still retain some relevance, and reviews notwithstanding, the movie was a box office disaster at the time. Production spanned the release of *The Jazz Singer*, and, with talking pictures all the rage, silent movies were dying a painful death. Often, talking scenes would be supplemented to a completed film in a bid to compete with the industry's newest innovation—and this was the case with *The Godless Girl*, to which some synched dialogue was added under the direction of Fritz Feld, as DeMille had already moved on to his next project.

The changes made little difference; the movie was one of DeMille's biggest flops, and many of the cast members found that their career's suffered as a result. For Marie Prevost this was a bitter blow, and she made only two more films as the decade drew to a close: *The Flying Fool* and *Divorce Made Easy*.

Divorce Made Easy was actually a "talkie"—Marie's first. Reports suggested that she had a Brooklyn "nasal whine." However, not only was she Canadian her voice actually translated well into talking films. There could be little doubt that her acting skills were subtle enough for her career to at least continue if not necessarily flourish.

However, the voice was accompanied—as could be seen in *The Godless Girl*—by an increasingly fuller figure courtesy of her drinking. With no major studio contract, Marie—by now in her midthirties (even "officially" she was over thirty)—no longer possessed her slim physique and youth, attributes that seemed to outweigh actual talent in front of a camera.

Another contributing factor in Marie's decline was the onset of the Great Depression, and the harder life became, the more Marie drank to ease her pain. And the more she drank, the less likely she was to be offered work—let alone a starring role or a contract. It was a vicious circle, and a whole combination of diverse circumstances resulted in downward spiral and a cycle that Marie simply couldn't break.

UP IN SMOKE

On page 76 is an image of Marie in *The Godless Girl*, which appeared in *Photoplay*. Marie's face looks quite thin, but her physical appearance—specifically her weight—was attracting more than a passing interest in the magazine gossip columns. During 1929, it was reported that Marie spent time in hospital after becoming ill through "severe dieting." *Picture-Play* commented: "You really aren't in polite society this year if you haven't collapsed from overwork and spent at least a week in a sanitarium. Betty Compson, Marie Prevost and Laura la Plante are the latest to go to hospital for a rest."

Her "desperate" attempts at losing weight to earn a part in a Cecil B. DeMille production mistakenly entitled "Madame Satin" by the *New York Daily News* [*the 1930 movie Madame Satan starred Kay Johnson*] were doomed because there was "too much poundage in evidence."

And in his "monthly Broadcast from Hollywood" feature in *Photoplay*, Cal York delivered this damning one-liner: "And IS Marie Prevost piling on the pounds!" I did read that the fictional name was created from California and New York, the locations of the magazine's editorial offices, and also that the column was considered one of the most respectful. Seriously?!

The changes in Marie's appearance were noticeable at the start of the new decade. *Party Girl* was the first 1930 release to feature Marie—although her name was somewhat curiously missing from the acting credits. By now, Marie was not only drinking to ease her emotional pain but she was also binge eating. However, Victor Halperin, who directed the movie, certainly didn't attempt to disguise Marie's weight gain. Right at the start of the film, an evidently naked Diana—Marie's role—was lying on a massage table being well and truly pummeled by an intimidating Louise Carver. Marie is later shown dressed only in black lingerie, wobbling unflatteringly courtesy of a vibrating machine.

A "party girl" was essentially a prostitute, so clearly certain aspects of the film were going to be fairly controversial. In actual fact, the movie was banned in Britain for a staggering seventy-three years.

The plot centered around Jay Rountree (played by Douglas Fairbanks Jr.) who found himself trapped into an unwanted marriage by a scheming Leeda Cather, played by the former model Judith Barrie—whose film career spanned just three years (1930-1932) and five movies.

In this film, Rountree's "real" love interest was Ellen Powell, played by the ill-fated—how many times have I used that phrase?—Jeanette Loff, whose demise in 1942 was caused by ammonia poisoning.

Party Girl opened with a screening just after midnight on New Year's Day, but for all the hype or notoriety, I didn't think this was a particularly good film. Notwithstanding the poor sound quality, the story doesn't really grab the audience's interest—although the subject matter may well have enticed viewers to cinemas—and the ending is particularly weak.

As for Marie, well the days when she was hired for being a beautiful young starlet were long gone, as was the effortless sexuality of her mid-to-late twenties.

She undoubtedly retained her comic timing, but the parts she was now being given were loud, fast-talking, and brash women, perhaps confident enough in their own skin to accept the way they looked. In reality, the former flapper was now being paraded—even ridiculed—in a way that is actually quite uncomfortable to watch. But I suppose it paid the bills.

Marie's next film was the Frank Capra-directed *Ladies of Leisure*. Marie reportedly lost "fifteen pounds in fourteen treatments by a masseuse," yet the *Picture-Play* correspondent deemed "she was overweight in [*the*] picture." That said, contrary to the opinion of others, her voice had a "winning naturalness."

The sad fact was that however Marie's performances were perceived, it was becoming increasingly evident that she was now expected to play her size for laughs.

Three more movies followed: *Sweethearts on Parade*, *War Nurse*—which starred Anita Page, who passed away as recently as 2008, reportedly aged ninety-eight—and *Paid*, in which Marie appeared alongside Joan Crawford. It is quite interesting to note that there had been three previous screen versions of this story (1916, 1917, and 1923), all of which were entitled *Within the Law*—this is actually the title given in *IMDb*. A further adaptation was recorded in 1939 with Ruth Hussey taking Joan Crawford's role of Mary Turner, and Rita Johnson playing Marie's part of Agnes "Aggie" Lynch.

Irrespective of how Marie's career was—or rather wasn't—progressing, 1930 was another incredibly tough year away from the film studios. On March 27, the *Border Cities Star* reported that Marie had been admitted to a Hollywood hospital for an operation for the "recurrence of an old ailment." It appears that Marie believed that she had become ill through dieting for a possible film part. Her physician disagreed and "ordered her to the hospital."

On April 8, the *News Dispatch* gave a further update on the actress's condition:

> *Marie Prevost goes home tomorrow from the hospital whence she went a week or so ago for an operation. Marie has certainly had her share of illness. Four or five ear operations is not too pleasant. Her ear trouble goes back sundry years when she was a Mack Sennett bathing beauty and traipsed in comedy after comedy making water scenes at any and all hours.*
>
> *Marie incidentally has lost quite a bit of weight and is said to have dieted to slim proportions.*

Then, just to nicely round off the year, on December 15, came the news of a serious fire, which had destroyed the homes and belongings of as many as "18 motion picture players" in Malibu Beach—I think you have probably guessed the identity of one of the victims already.

The fire began following a mysterious "blast" at half past two in the morning and spread rapidly from house to house, fanned by a northerly wind. Seemingly, many occupants were forced to evacuate their homes still wearing their night clothes, and it took fire crews three hours to bring the blaze under control. There was some thought that inadequate firefighting apparatus was partially responsible for the length of time it took to deal with the fire, although other reports suggested that changes in wind direction had posed problems for those tackling the fire.

An immediate, but tentative, estimate of $800,000 was placed on the loss. As well as the structural damage and loss of personal possessions, a number of expensive cars were also destroyed. Apart from Marie—who had been "sleeping blissfully when the bonfire began"—I had only heard of one of the other "stars" directly affected by the fire and that was Louise Fazenda (who had appeared with Marie in the film *Bobbed Hair*).

According to *Motion Picture* magazine, Marie rushed out of her house, where she was comforted by Buster Collier. He apparently said to her: "Never mind darling, it won't take long to build another one." An hour later they were still both standing in the road, with Marie berating Collier that she "could have saved so-and-so if you had just let me do as I wanted to do." Another article suggested that Collier had "dashed up and down coupling and uncoupling hose[s]; sometimes the wrong ones."

A couple of things here: whatever the state of Marie's career, it does seem that she wasn't short of money, and here is the first mention of her current beau, Buster Collier. His relationship with the actress had not escaped the noted gossip columnist Louella Parsons during 1929: "One of the new crushes involves Buster Collier and Marie Prevost, Phyllis Haver's chum. There are those who intimate Marie is matrimonially inclined, but others are less convinced that the Prevost-Collier romance is anything so permanent."

Buster was actually the nickname of William Collier Jr., which was the adopted name of Charles F Gall Jr.—still with me? Collier and Marie were best man and bridesmaid respectively at the 1930 wedding of cowboy actor Hoot Gibson to Sally Eilers, and the couple were "spotted" still together at *Sebastian's Cotton Club* in February 1933, according to another of Louella Parsons's columns.

Anyway, back to the fire. Marie reportedly didn't leave her burning home empty-handed: she saved an umbrella and an arm full of books. Her main losses were given as $15,000 and "some invaluable miniatures."

One magazine article claimed that Marie was lucky because "her house didn't burn to the ground"—arguably splitting hairs, based on photographic evidence—but in actual fact, because everything that remained was "so charred and defaced that it was ruined forever," Marie was the only resident forced to pay to have the remains of her home removed before rebuilding.

Harsh.

In March 1931, Marie featured in the "Snoopings" section of the *Milwaukee Sentinel*—she had been spotted "buying furniture for her new Malibu house . . . also fire insurance."

The *Toledo News Bee* of September 8, 1931, revealed that Marie was an avid collector of first edition books, and that "letters of regret had poured in on her" after volumes worth $4,000 had been lost in the blaze.

And finally, some ten years later, there were a few lines about the fire in the *Reading Eagle* (July 29, 1941) when a reporter remembered "when the late Marie Prevost broke through fire lines on the night of the big Malibu blaze to rescue a favorite picture of her current boyfriend."

Which was presumably hidden inside the umbrella. . . .

As you can plainly see, the *Reading Eagle* quote gives away the fact that Marie's life would end sooner rather than later—and with that rather sobering thought, we shall move on.

THE LAST DIE

Although Marie found plenty of work in 1931, the lead roles had disappeared and she was now playing bit parts with few lines—and presumably earning less money as a result. As you will see, she did appear alongside some of the biggest names of the era, but I doubt that was of much consolation.

Early in the year, Dorothy Manners of *Motion Picture* magazine wrote an article entitled "138 Lbs. Ringside!" which was concerned primarily with the near three-stone increase in Marie's weight since her Bathing Beauty days.

The article started like this: "When Marie Prevost did that big climbing-the-stairs number in *Ladies of Leisure*, she hoisted about 138 pounds of the cutest 'comeback' Hollywood has witnessed in many a day."

Marie's appearances in *War Nurse* and *Within the Law* [*Paid*] were described as a "chubby return" and although the inference was that Marie was comfortable with her weight, her eating and drinking habits suggested otherwise.

Marie's 1931 movies were *Gentleman's Fate* (with Anita Page), followed by *It's a Wise Child*—a comedy starring Marion Davies. Then came *The Good Bad Girl*, *West of the Rockies*—in which Marie had a starring role, but the film was actually made in 1929 as *All Faces West*, but not released until 1931, complete with talking prologue. Next was *Sporting Blood* (which starred Clark Gable), followed by *Waiting for the Bride*—also known as *The Runaround*, or *Waiting at the Church*—*Reckless Living*, *The Lullaby* (or *The Sin of Madelon Claudet*), and *Hell Divers* (also with Gable), which completed her year's work.

Marie's appearance as Dot in the 1932 movie *Three Wise Girls* saw her perform alongside one of my screen idols: the stunning Jean Harlow.

Marie is excellent in this film. It's so sad that she no longer fitted the Hollywood stereotype—let's be honest, she may have put on a bit of weight, but she was far from being "fat," and her experience of bringing quality comedy to the big screen was still very much in evidence. So was the difference between supporting roles and top billing, success and failure, really nothing more than a few pounds?

The final member of this astute triumvirate was Mae Clarke who had previously appeared in *The Good Bad Girl*, but whose main claim to cinematic fame was arguably having a pre-code grapefruit thrust into her face by James Cagney in what was a strangely uncredited appearance in another Jean Harlow picture, *The Public Enemy* (in 1931). Sadly though, just as with Cecil B. DeMille's involvement in *The Godless Girl*, Jean Harlow's presence could do little to save *Three Wise Girls* from bombing at the cinemas.

My magazine collection is all but exhausted—Marie's face was rapidly disappearing from the pages of the various trade and fan publications—but I do have a copy of *Three Wise Girls*, so here is a screen still of Marie (as Dot) and la belle Ms. Harlow as Cassie.

Only three more films followed in 1932: *Carnival Boat* (with Ginger Rogers), *Slightly Married*, and a twenty-minute short entitled *Hesitating Love*, which starred Louise Fazenda. The parts may have been drying up, but as this excerpt from an article about *Slightly Married* shows, Marie was still turning out good performances, despite all her off-screen issues: "Miss Prevost has gained weight. But the loss of box office appeal through the ability to fill a bathing suit just so has not taken with it the young lady's acting ability. She comes through in grand style as a straight comedian."

Those personal troubles were further compounded in October 1932, when an insurance company took legal action against Marie for non-payment of just over $600 in respect of fire and car policies.

By now, Marie was working on a freelance basis and, with no regular contract income, she had to accept almost any work. By the end of 1933, her career had almost come full circle as her appearance in *Only Yesterday* was uncredited; the movie was based on Stefan Zweig's novel *Briefe einer Unbekannten* [*Letter from an Unknown Woman*], although as far as being credited for his work, Zweig suffered the same fate as Marie Prevost.

For the record, the four movies in which Marie featured earlier in 1933 were *Rock-a-Bye Cowboy*, *Parole Girl*, *The Eleventh Commandment*, and *Pick Me Up*. During the year (and on page 86), she also appeared alongside Buster Collier in a photograph from the June issue of *New Movie* magazine—a sad moment, as this is my last image from my clearly limited collection. Marie's slide down the Hollywood pecking order was essentially completed—with a fairly loud thud—in 1934 when she appeared in absolutely no films at all.

In contrast to the glowing reviews, the papers would now include an occasional paragraph to tell how Marie had shed a few pounds and was available for work. The truth about her weight loss was not so much about dieting rather than she was simply not eating. Her financial situation became precarious: Marie was forced to sell her Malibu home, and she took up residence in a small apartment at 6230 Afton Place in Hollywood.

Marie was, however, back in work again in 1935. The film was *Keystone Hotel*, a two-reel comedy produced by her former employer Warner Brothers, and it starred other Mack Sennett alumni such as Ben Turpin and Chester Conklin.

In many ways, this was a standard Sennett short filmed nearly two decades too late: the plot—such as it was—revolved around Turpin as Count Drewa Blanc, who had arrived at the Keystone Hotel to judge a beauty contest.

As he got out of his car, a photographer yelled: "Look straight at the camera, Count!"

I'm sure he tried. . . .

The Count was "encouraged" by the chief of police, the Mayor, and a local gangster to vote for their respective wife, wife, and presumably moll, but he contrived to award first prize to an old woman who had only been on stage helping to adjust the ladies' dresses.

"How dare you give it to her when I should get it?" exclaimed one of the contestants, and "get it" she duly did, in the form of a pie in the face. The descent into a pie-throwing fight involving pretty much anyone and everyone was quick, fairly predictable, but still quite funny anyway, and the former Bathing Beauty was not afforded any escape as the festivities continued.

It's something of an irony that this concoction of marshmallow paste, stewed blackberries, and apricots—apparently the combination splattered effectively—was probably the closest Marie had come to eating anything for quite a while. Here is how the *Indian Express* dated July 20, 1935, reported the meeting between pie and film star: "'Come on, get ready. Yours is the next take', orders the director—and then 'Splash'—Marie Prevost 'takes' a gooey blackberry pie right in the nose. It smears her from brow to chin, the juice trickling across her arms and shoulders."

The same article stated that Marie was "more buxom than formerly," but *The Leader Post* of June 15, 1935, said: "Having taken off forty pounds in the last year, Marie looks every bit as well as she did in the old days."

But the last word on this film, and the pies in particular, just has to come from Ben Turpin: "These pies are from a totally different family tree than the ones I used to know . . . and I was personally acquainted with them all."

Curiously, seeing as Marie had revisited her comedy roots, so roots of another kind surfaced around that time as press stories claimed Marie had "received word from Glasgow" advising that she had inherited a Scottish estate, ownership of which had seemingly passed to her from her great grandmother.

I question the truth behind this for two reasons: firstly, any such inheritance would surely have solved many of Marie's problems instantly; and secondly the story was dated April 1....

Marie's next screen appearance was in *Hands Across the Table* in which she played Nona, alongside the talented, beautiful, yet also ill-fated—how many more times?—Carole Lombard, who portrayed Regi. Both were manicurists, and Regi was on the lookout for a man—a rich man—but as you'd probably expect, that's not quite how things turn out.

In one particular scene, Regi was about to go on a date when she gets the hiccups. A relevant, albeit random, snippet appeared in the *Ottawa Citizen* dated August 22, 1935, which suggested that six takes of the scene were shot, during which Carole "hicced" and Marie appeared with a glass of water. On the seventh take, Marie brought beer instead of the water, which Carole still drank, causing her—at least according to the article—to "get the hiccups for real."

Reviews of Marie's performance were mainly positive, yet she only made two movies in 1935—in actual fact it was now two in two years—and by 1936, it appears that she was relying on handouts from friends, presumably to satisfy her need for alcohol.

Marie's dramatic and none-too-healthy means of losing weight seemed to have paid professional dividends, however. A much-quoted *New York Times* article entitled "Sometimes They Do Come Back" stated:

> *In the studio restaurant at Warners there is an 'Old-Timers Tables' [sic] that is reserved, in tacit arrangement, for the group of former stars who like to talk over together their halcyon days. A few weeks ago, Marie Prevost sat down at the table. The siren of Mack Sennett days had been successful with a reducing course and had got herself a job as a contract player. She was put to work almost immediately, in a small part in 'The Bengal Tiger'...*
>
> *Miss Prevost is unbilled in 'The Bengal Tiger'. She has only three lines to say, and those are short ones. But she is back at work, skipping arc-light cables and dodging camera dollies on the set once more.*
>
> *A few more parts of a few lines each and the studio may find bigger and better things for her to do.*

By the time *Bengal Tiger* was released, Marie had already appeared in *Tango* and *Thirteen Hours by Air*. An uncredited role as a receptionist in *Cain and Mabel* followed before Marie appeared as a waitress named Elsie in the car racing film *Ten Laps to Go*.

And so it was, surrounded by food and with much biting of lower lip, that Marie Prevost said farewell to the big screen.

At this point, Peggy (Marjorie) reappears—as indeed does the salt cellar.

She had apparently written to Marie "several times during 1936, but never got more than a brief postcard in reply." Peggy supposedly told her husband that they really should visit her sister. They didn't get round to it, and in fact, Peggy never saw Marie alive again.

A WONDERFUL FRIEND

Marie Prevost died in January 1937—the date is likely to be the twenty-first. Her demise was as tragic as it was pitiful.

There had been a number of complaints from residents in the Afton Place building, about the incessant barking from inside Marie's apartment—Marie owned a dachshund called Maxie.

Repeated knocks on her door went unanswered, but the dog continued barking. There was a note on the door stating: "Please do not knock on the door more than once as it makes my dog bark. If I am in I will hear you as I am not deaf."

Well Marie was in—and whilst she may not have been deaf, she was most definitely dead. This is how the *Los Angeles Times* of January 24, 1937, announced Marie's passing:

> **One-Time Queen of Sennett Beauties Victim of Heart Attack in Modest Home**
>
> Marie Prevost, 38 years of age, once reigning queen of the Sennett bathing beauties, was found dead yesterday in her modest single apartment at 6230 Afton Place, Hollywood. Apparently dead two-days, her body was found clothed and face down on a folding bed.
>
> Whining at the bedside was her pet dachshund, Maxie, and teeth marks on the actress' body indicated animal had tugged at his mistress in an attempt to arouse her.

The article further set the scene by describing how two gas heaters were burning under the open window in Marie's "tiny" kitchen, and that a number of empty whisky bottles lay in the sink. Police Detective Lieutenants Stambler and Sanderson explained that, whist Marie's apartment was untidy, there were no obvious signs of violence nor a suspicious death. In fact, the officers declared that Marie had undoubtedly died as a result of a heart attack, although the body would be taken to the morgue where an autopsy would be performed.

It was suggested that Mrs. Henrietta Jenks, who was the manager of the apartment block, had become concerned at the lack of noise or activity from Marie's particular apartment and she apparently sent a houseboy named William Bogle to investigate. He used a passkey to gain entry and found Marie's motionless body on the bed. She had taken off her shoes and stockings and "drawn a robe over her, apparently as one would do before taking a nap."

Mrs. Jenks's husband, Harry, called the police, and Bogle later stated that he'd last seen Marie alive the previous Wednesday, when he'd cleaned her apartment. On that same day, Marie had spoken with a teenager named Bernard Weiss in a local delicatessen. He claimed Marie had told him that she'd "redeemed a $2.50 check which had been returned by the bank" and that "she had been in Laguna Beach for two months."

The paper reported that Marie was heavily in debt, although a note was found indicating Joan Crawford had lent her money to help her through what was described as a "difficult period." When her body was found, Marie's purse contained $100, and she was believed to have paid her rent in advance.

There is a picture of the death scene that is readily available on the internet. I presume it's genuine—it's not overly or gratuitously graphic—but in a literal sense it's certainly pathetic. An actress, once right at—or at least very close to—the top of her profession, now lay lifeless. Marie's body had simply waved the white flag after being bombarded by alcohol and starved of nourishment for too long. Some reports suggested Marie had taken her own life, but this was essentially the inevitable end to ritual bodily abuse in a vain bid to regain the figure that she hoped might attract the attention of a film studio or director.

There are one or two comments that need to be supplemented to the *LA Times* article: Marie was not thirty-eight when she died, she had recently passed her fortieth birthday.

The marks on Marie's legs were Maxie's futile attempts at rousing his mistress. Suggestions that Marie's corpse had been "half-eaten" by the dog—as put forward by Kenneth Anger in *Hotel Babylon*—are absurdly wide of the mark. And I'm devoting just as little space to the singer Nick Lowe's song *Marie Provost*—he couldn't even be bothered to spell her name correctly.

Sadly, the loyal pet's fate was to be put to sleep soon after.

The report mentions an autopsy. One of those involved was Dr. Frank R. Webb, the assistant county autopsy surgeon, whose signature appeared on the death certificate. He gave the cause of death as acute alcoholism—not the malnutrition that some sources have claimed. The certificate also stated the date of death as January 20— this is clearly a presumption or educated guess—and incorrectly named Frank Prevost as Marie's father.

Marie's funeral was held at Hollywood Memorial Cemetery—it was reported that her body was later cremated and the ashes may have been placed with those of her mother—and was paid for by Joan Crawford (with whom Marie featured in *Paid/Within the Law*). On hearing of Marie's passing, Ms Crawford said: "We were good friends. She had only to ask and I would gladly have given her help, money, or other assistance that she needed. She was a wonderful friend and a great comedy actress."

Lovely words.

According to Peggy, Joan Crawford felt somehow responsible for Marie's death and was inconsolable—to the extent that two days' filming had to be canceled because she was too distraught to be on set. Perhaps—but condiments still on stand-by.

Amongst those who gathered to pay their respects were Barbara Stanwyck, Mack Sennett, Douglas Fairbanks Jr., Clark Gable, Wallace Beery, King Baggot, Robert Young, and Fred MacMurray.

Marie left an estate worth just $300—a sad fact on which to end the story of the life of a beautiful and vibrant young woman whose cinematic dream turned into a nightmare escape from which came at the highest possible price.

ON REFLECTION

And so another Hollywood candle was extinguished far too early. There are relatively few sources of information about the life of Marie Prevost and it is clear that some of those that do exist are flawed; all of which means that trying to unravel Marie's life is no simple task. But offering an opinion as to the character of this young woman is much harder—albeit the ability to produce evidence to disagree with any considered subjective viewpoint is likely to be every bit as difficult.

I hope I have been able to weed out some of the more obvious inaccuracies from the publicly available material, but what of Marie?

Losing a parent in any circumstances is tough to deal with, but Marie was denied the chance to be raised by her natural father by his most unnatural death when she was just one year old. The fact that Marie would later lose her mother in violent circumstances must have placed an even bigger emotional burden on her shoulders.

The mysterious disappearance into the shadows of Frank Prevost and the apparent creation of Eric Prevost are puzzling, but I guess the Hollywood wheels take some stopping once they've started turning. Perhaps the lack of a father figure is one reason for what seems to be a poor choice in men; both her marriages failed, but unlike some other actresses in a similar position, I found hardly any rumors of Marie seeking some sort of no-strings solace in the arms of other men.

Despite no formal theatre training, Marie made the transition from Bathing Beauty to star both quickly and seemingly effortlessly. Her looks had opened the door, but there was no denying her talent as an actress; she had superb facial expression and was blessed with natural comic timing that would be evident in both silent and talking movies.

I wonder quite how things would have turned out had her mother not made that fateful car journey in 1926. But without the predetermined denial of these "what ifs," I guess the lives of performers such as Marie Prevost wouldn't be anywhere near as interesting or compelling.

A grieving Marie chose a path that put into motion a series of actions and events that would inevitably lead to her own reclusive death. People cared about Marie—arguably more than she cared about herself.

Film producers wanted young, slim, and pretty. By her mid-thirties, Marie arguably only possessed the last of those "essentials," but she was evidently prepared to go to any lengths to rediscover the flapper who had wowed movie audiences in the 1920s.

That goal was clearly more important than the means of getting there, and Marie basically abused the body that had helped her achieve fame and fortune until it gave up—by that time, the fame had subsided and the fortune had gone.

The impression I formed about Marie was that she possessed a genuine and kind heart as well as an almost childlike naivety, which needed the support of her family—her mother.

Without that foundation, Marie was exposed and quite probably out of her depth. Alcohol might temporarily numb the pain and postpone dealing with real-life issues, but whereas the effects of drink may wear off—even if only briefly—the problems would always be waiting.

For me, it wasn't just her alcohol dependency that stripped Marie Prevost of her dignity, it was the film industry—the unwritten need or pressure to conform. Hollywood basically chewed up and spat out a normal decent young woman, safe in the knowledge that there'd always be a willing replacement waiting in the wings.

I absolutely accept that my thoughts may be wide of the mark, but in the time I have spent reading and writing about Marie Prevost, as well as watching a number of her film appearances, I can't help but feel she was a victim of circumstance—a young woman who seemed to have everything but for whom fate was always one step ahead.

God bless, Marie x.

BIBLIOGRAPHY, SOURCES & ACKNOWLEDGEMENTS

What follows is a comprehensive list of the books, newspapers, magazines, and web sites that have formed part of my research for this book. All the images are from magazines, photographs, cards, and DVDs that I have purchased, however, I unreservedly acknowledge the copyright of any individual owner of material adapted within these pages.

Books:
Hollywood Goes Shopping by David Desser
Hotel Babylon by Kenneth Anger
Howard Hughes: Hell's Angel by Darwin Porter
Inside the Hollywood Fan Magazine: A History of Star Makers, Fabricators, and Gossip Mongers by Anthony Slide
King Baggot: A Biography and Filmography of the First King of the Movies by Sally Dumeaux
Mack Sennett's Fun Factory by Brent Walker
Stardust and Shadows by Charles Foster

Magazines:
The Flapper Magazine (May 1922)
Mack Sennett Weekly (25/06/17)
Motion Picture Magazine (various)
Motion Picture Classic (Feb 1922)
Motion Picture World (1923)
New Movie (various)
Picture-Play (various)
Photoplay (various)
Time Magazine (23/08/23)

Newspapers:
Atlanta Constitution (02/10/21)
Berkeley Daily Gazette (05/01/26, 06/02/26)
Border-Cities Star (27/03/30)
Brisbane Courier (04/12/29)
Evening Independent (29/11/24, 30/11/28)
Indian Express (20/07/35)
Los Angeles Mirror (1923)
Los Angeles Times (12/08/23, 10/02/26, 24/01/37)
Milwaukee Journal (16/10/27, 13/01/29)
Milwaukee Sentinel (02/09/28, March 1931)
New York Times (30/11/1897, 03/08/25)
New Zealand Truth
News Dispatch (08/04/30)

Ottawa Citizen (22/08/35)
Pittsburgh Post Gazette (05/04/28)
Pittsburgh Press (29/06/24, 17/04/26, 1932)
Reading Eagle (29/07/41)
San Francisco Call (15/02/22)
Saskatoon Star Phoenix (14/06/30)
Southeast Missourian (20/11/25)
Toledo News Bee (08/09/31)
Tonawanda News (12/01/55)
Youngstown Vindicator (06/02/26, 27/07/35)

Web Sites:
familysearch.org
findagrave.com
flapperjane.com
freepages.genealogy.rootsweb.ancestry.com
imdb.com
sbbn.wordpress.com
shebloggedbynight.com
(The Marie Prevost Project – The Racket 1928 (09/02/10)
(The Marie Prevost Project – Party Girl 1930 (29/03/10)
(The Marie Prevost Project #1 - Those Bitter Sweets 1915 (10/11/10)
(The Gone Too Soon Blogathon: Marie Prevost 10/03/12)
silentera.com
silentsaregolden.com
silverscreenoasis.com
theloudestvoice.tumblr.com
wikipedia.org
youtube.com

www.ingramcontent.com/pod-product-compliance
Lightning Source LLC
Chambersburg PA
CBHW071625170426

43195CB00038B/2135